MATHEMATICS POWER LEARNING FOR CHILDREN

WORKBOOK TWO

Everard Barrett

CONTEXTUAL MATHEMATICS TEACHING METHODOLOGY

Professor B Enterprises, Inc.
P. O. Box 2079
Duluth, GA 30096
www.profb.com

FOURTH EDITION REVISED

Copyrights and acknowledgments

Editor
Everard Barrett

Production Manager
Veda Barrett

Cover Art
Charles J. Berger

Publisher
Professor B Enterprises, Inc.
P. O. Box 2079
Duluth, GA 30096
www.profb.com

Copyright © Everard Barrett, 1993
All rights reserved.

Published in the United States by Professor B Enterprises, Inc. Portions of this workbook were previously published under the following titles:

1. *Teach Me, Professor B*. Copyright © Everard Barrett, 1987. All rights reserved.
2. *Personal Discovery*. Copyright © Everard Barrett, 1979. All rights reserved.
3. *Barrett Educational Science Techniques*. Copyright © Everard Barrett, 1978. All rights reserved.
4. *Achieving "Fifth Grade Math" As a Second Grader*. Copyright © Everard Barrett, 1977. All rights reserved.

No part of this publication may be reproduced or transmitted in any form or by any means, electronic or mechanical, including photocopy, recording, or any information storage and retrieval system, without permission in writing from both the copyright owner and the publisher of this book.

FOURTH EDITION REVISED

ISBN 1-883324-05-X

Printed in the United States of America

Table of Contents

		PAGE
FACILITY EXERCISES **#1**	SOLVING WORD PROBLEMS	1
FACILITY EXERCISES **#2**	MASTERING THE MULTIPLICATION FACTS QUICKLY	2
FACILITY EXERCISES **#3**	MASTERING THE MULTIPLICATION FACTS QUICKLY	3
FACILITY EXERCISES **#4**	MASTERING THE MULTIPLICATION FACTS QUICKLY	4
FACILITY EXERCISES **#5**	MASTERING THE MULTIPLICATION FACTS QUICKLY	5
FACILITY EXERCISES **#6**	MASTERING THE MULTIPLICATION FACTS QUICKLY	6
FACILITY EXERCISES **#7**	MASTERING THE MULTIPLICATION FACTS QUICKLY	7
FACILITY EXERCISES **#8**	MIXED PRACTICE	8
FACILITY EXERCISES **#9**	MASTERING THE MULTIPLICATION FACTS QUICKLY	11
FACILITY EXERCISES **#10**	MASTERING THE MULTIPLICATION FACTS QUICKLY	13
FACILITY EXERCISES **#11**	MASTERING THE MULTIPLICATION FACTS QUICKLY	15
FACILITY EXERCISES **#12**	MASTERING THE MULTIPLICATION FACTS QUICKLY	17
FACILITY EXERCISES **#13**	MASTERING THE MULTIPLICATION FACTS QUICKLY	19
FACILITY EXERCISES **#14**	MASTERING THE MULTIPLICATION FACTS QUICKLY	21
FACILITY EXERCISES **#15**	MASTERING THE MULTIPLICATION FACTS QUICKLY	23
FACILITY EXERCISES **#16**	MASTERING THE MULTIPLICATION FACTS QUICKLY	25
FACILITY EXERCISES **#17**	MASTERING THE MULTIPLICATION FACTS QUICKLY	27
FACILITY EXERCISES **#18**	MASTERING THE MULTIPLICATION FACTS QUICKLY	29
FACILITY EXERCISES **#19**	MASTERING THE MULTIPLICATION FACTS QUICKLY	31
FACILITY EXERCISES **#20**	MASTERING THE MULTIPLICATION FACTS QUICKLY	32
FACILITY EXERCISES **#21**	MASTERING THE MULTIPLICATION FACTS QUICKLY	33
FACILITY EXERCISES **#22**	LINKING MULTIPLICATION AND DIVISION FACTS	34
FACILITY EXERCISES **#23**	LINKING MULTIPLICATION AND DIVISION FACTS	38
FACILITY EXERCISES **#24**	LINKING MULTIPLICATION AND DIVISION FACTS	40
FACILITY EXERCISES **#25**	PREPARING FOR DIVISION WITH REMAINDER	42
FACILITY EXERCISES **#26**	SHORT DIVISION WITH REMAINDER	44
FACILITY EXERCISES **#27**	MIXED PRACTICE	48
FACILITY EXERCISES **#28**	MORE MULTIPLICATION FACTS	50
FACILITY EXERCISES **#29**	PREPARING FOR MULTIPLICATION BY TWO OR MORE DIGITS	51
FACILITY EXERCISES **#30**	PREPARING FOR MULTIPLICATION BY TWO OR MORE DIGITS	53
FACILITY EXERCISES **#31**	PREPARING FOR MULTIPLICATION BY TWO OR MORE DIGITS	54
FACILITY EXERCISES **#32**	PREPARING FOR MULTIPLICATION BY TWO OR MORE DIGITS	55
FACILITY EXERCISES **#33**	TELLING THE TRUTH WHEN MULTIPLYING WHOLE NUMBERS	56
FACILITY EXERCISES **#34**	TELLING THE TRUTH WHEN MULTIPLYING WHOLE NUMBERS	58
FACILITY EXERCISES **#35**	MIXED PRACTICE	60
FACILITY EXERCISES **#36**	TELLING THE TRUTH WHEN MULTIPLYING WHOLE NUMBERS	62
FACILITY EXERCISES **#37**	SOLVING WORD PROBLEMS	65
FACILITY EXERCISES **#38**	TELLING THE TRUTH ABOUT LONG DIVISION	67
FACILITY EXERCISES **#39**	MIXED PRACTICE	70
FACILITY EXERCISES **#40**	TELLING THE TRUTH ABOUT LONG DIVISION	73
FACILITY EXERCISES **#41**	TELLING THE TRUTH ABOUT LONG DIVISION	78
FACILITY EXERCISES **#42**	SOLVING WORD PROBLEMS	80
FACILITY EXERCISES **#43**	MULTIPLES	85

Table of Contents (continued)

		PAGE
FACILITY EXERCISES **#44**	FACTORS	86
FACILITY EXERCISES **#45**	MIXED PRACTICE	87
FACILITY EXERCISES **#46**	PRIME FACTORIZATION	90
FACILITY EXERCISES **#47**	FINDING ALL FACTORS OF A NUMBER	91
FACILITY EXERCISES **#48**	LEAST COMMON MULTIPLE	92
FACILITY EXERCISES **#49**	HIGHEST COMMON FACTOR	94
FACILITY EXERCISES **#50**	MIXED PRACTICE	96
FACILITY EXERCISES **#51**	USING PRIME FACTORIZATION TO FIND THE L.C.M.	99
FACILITY EXERCISES **#52**	USING PRIME FACTORIZATION TO FIND THE H.C.F.	100
FACILITY EXERCISES **#53**	INTRODUCTION TO FRACTIONS	101
FACILITY EXERCISES **#54**	FAMILIES OF EQUIVALENT FRACTIONS	103
FACILITY EXERCISES **#55**	MIXED PRACTICE	106
FACILITY EXERCISES **#56**	FAMILIES OF EQUIVALENT FRACTIONS	110
FACILITY EXERCISES **#57**	FAMILIES OF EQUIVALENT FRACTIONS	112
FACILITY EXERCISES **#58**	REDUCING FRACTIONS TO LOWEST TERMS	114
FACILITY EXERCISES **#59**	REDUCING FRACTIONS TO LOWEST TERMS	115
FACILITY EXERCISES **#60**	REDUCING FRACTIONS TO LOWEST TERMS	117
FACILITY EXERCISES **#61**	ADDING AND SUBTRACTING WITH FRACTIONS	119
FACILITY EXERCISES **#62**	ADDING AND SUBTRACTING WITH FRACTIONS	123
FACILITY EXERCISES **#63**	MIXED PRACTICE	124
FACILITY EXERCISES **#64**	TRANSFORMING IMPROPER FRACTIONS TO MIXED NUMBERS	128
FACILITY EXERCISES **#65**	TRANSFORMING IMPROPER FRACTIONS TO MIXED NUMBERS	129
FACILITY EXERCISES **#66**	TRANSFORMING MIXED NUMBERS TO IMPROPER FRACTIONS	130
FACILITY EXERCISES **#67**	TRANSFORMING MIXED NUMBERS TO IMPROPER FRACTIONS	131
FACILITY EXERCISES **#68**	ADDING AND SUBTRACTING WITH MIXED NUMBERS	132
FACILITY EXERCISES **#69**	TRANSFORMING MIXED NUMBERS	135
FACILITY EXERCISES **#70**	"EXCHANGE" IN SUBTRACTION WITH MIXED NUMBERS	136
FACILITY EXERCISES **#71**	ADDING AND SUBTRACTING WITH FRACTIONS AND MIXED NUMBERS	137
FACILITY EXERCISES **#72**	MIXED PRACTICE	140

MASTERING THE MULTIPLICATION FACTS QUICKLY
FACILITY EXERCISES #5

Do the examples below.

(1) $6{,}395{,}408{,}172 \times 2$

(2) $1{,}578{,}409{,}362 \times 3$

(3) $5{,}418{,}270{,}936 \times 2$

(4) $6{,}483{,}504{,}791 \times 3$

(5) $9{,}154{,}376{,}802 \times 3$

(6) $3{,}852{,}740{,}916 \times 3$

(7) $2{,}486{,}594{,}713 \times 3$

(8) $6{,}809{,}537{,}426 \times 3$

(9) $6{,}472{,}581{,}930 \times 3$

(10) $5{,}938{,}241{,}076 \times 3$

(11) $1{,}498{,}625{,}307 \times 3$

(12) $1{,}498{,}625{,}307 + 1{,}498{,}625{,}307 + 1{,}498{,}625{,}307$

(13) $5{,}176{,}204{,}937 + 5{,}176{,}204{,}937 + 5{,}176{,}204{,}937$

(14) $5{,}176{,}204{,}937 \times 3$

(15) $8{,}630{,}591{,}247 + 8{,}630{,}591{,}247 + 8{,}630{,}591{,}247$

(16) $8{,}630{,}591{,}247 \times 3$

MASTERING THE MULTIPLICATION FACTS QUICKLY
FACILITY EXERCISES #6

Do the examples below.

(1) 3,701,492,865
x 2

(2) 3,701,492,865
x 3

(3) 3,701,492,865
x 3

(4) 3,701,492,865
3,701,492,865
3,701,492,865
+ 3,701,492,865

(5) 4,372,095,168
x 4

(6) 5,732,869,104
x 4

(7) 7,018,329,546
x 4

(8) 8,470,936,152
x 4

(9) 3,917,260,584
x 2

(10) 3,940,857,162
x 3

(11) 3,917,260,584
x 4

(12) 2,589,302,476
x 4

(13) 1,593,047,286
1,593,047,286
1,593,047,286
+ 1,593,047,286

(14) 1,593,047,286
x 4

MASTERING THE MULTIPLICATION FACTS QUICKLY
FACILITY EXERCISES #7

Do the examples below.

(1) 6,483,504,791 x 4

(2) 3,852,740,916 x 4

(3) 9,154,376,802 x 4

(4) 2,486,594,713 x 4

(5) 5,840,167,938 x 2

(6) 5,840,167,938 x 3

(7) 6,809,537,426 x 4

(8) 6,472,581,930 x 4

(9) 5,938,241,076 x 4

(10) 1,069,547,283 x 4

(11) 9,876,543,210 x 2

(12) 9,876,543,210 x 3

(13) 4,690,581,273
4,690,581,273
4,690,581,273
+ 4,690,581,273

(14) 8,253,901,674
8,253,901,674
8,253,901,674
+ 8,253,901,674

(15) 4,690,581,273 x 4

(16) 8,253,901,674 x 4

FACILITY EXERCISES #8
Mixed Practice

Write your answers in the spaces provided.

1. Find answers to the examples below without use of fingers.

(a) **3 – 2 + 9 – 4 – 2 + 5 =** _____

(c) **3 + 3 + 3 – 2 – 2 – 2 + 4 =** _____

(b) **2 + 3 + 4 – 5 + 6 – 3 – 3 =** _____

(d) **2 + 2 + 3 – 6 + 4 + 3 – 5 =** _____

2. Do each addition and subtraction below. Check the answer to each subtraction.

(a)
```
  8,473,906
+ 6,795,897
```

(b)
```
  93,700,581
– 89,842,795
```

(c)
```
  9,748,637
+   957,285
```

(d)
```
  7,000,463
–   953,192
```

3. Start at zero and count by sixes to sixty.

4. Start at zero and count by sevens to seventy.

5. Start at zero and count by eights to eighty.

6. Start at zero and count by nines to ninety.

7. Count backward by sixes from sixty-five to five.

8. Start at four and count by sevens to seventy-four.

9. Read each numeral below:

(a) **600,000,000,000**

(b) **72,727,272,727,272**

(c) **30,303,030,303,030**

10. Name the number which each digit in 60,570,043,128 represents.

11. Name the value of each place in 60,570,043,128.

12. The number 570,043,128 is in

(a) which hundred-millions? ______________________

(b) which hundreds? ______________________

(c) which ten-thousands? ______________________

(d) which ones? ______________________

(e) which hundred-thousands? ______________________

(f) which millions? ______________________

(g) which tens? ______________________

(h) which thousands? ______________________

(i) which ten-millions? ______________________

13. Tell the truth as you do the addition and subtraction example below.

(a)
$$\begin{array}{r} 684{,}957 \\ +\ 862{,}946 \\ \hline \end{array}$$

(b)
$$\begin{array}{r} 605{,}008 \\ -\ 278{,}053 \\ \hline \end{array}$$

14. Find the missing numbers.

(a) _____ − 258 = 376

(b) 103 = _____ + 97

(c) _____ + 145 = 200

(d) 16 = 37 − _____

15. Add the following:

(a)	(b)
643	587
298	679
769	968
584	795
477	876
956	578
898	969
749	888
328	694
876	787
987	979
696	868
569	796
+ 777	+ 577

16. Do the following multiplications:

(a)

829,746
x 2

(b)

704,897
x 3

(c)

5,790,086
x 4

MASTERING THE MULTIPLICATION FACTS QUICKLY
FACILITY EXERCISES #9

Do the examples below.

(1) 4,372,095,168 x 5

(2) 5,732,869,104 x 5

(3) 4,756 x 2

(4) 4,756 x 3

(5) 4,756 x 4

(6) 4,756 x 5

(7) 7,018,329,546 x 5

(8) 8,470,936,152 x 5

(9) 6,537,489,210 x 5

(10) 1,785,049,623 x 5

(11) 658,497 x 2

(12) 658,497 x 3

(13) 658,497 x 4

(14) 658,497 x 5

(15) 7,018,329,546 x 5

(16) 8,470,936,152 x 5

(17)
```
  3,581,402,697
  3,581,402,697
  3,581,402,697
  3,581,402,697
+ 3,581,402,697
_______________
```

(18)
```
3, 581,402,697
           x 5
______________
```

(19)
```
6,048,317,259
          x 5
_____________
```

(20)
```
  6,048,317,259
  6,048,317,259
  6,048,317,259
  6,048,317,259
+ 6,048,317,259
_______________
```

MASTERING THE MULTIPLICATION FACTS QUICKLY
FACILITY EXERCISES #10

Do the examples below.

(1) 1,493,265,087 x 5

(2) 6,483,504,791 x 5

(3) 3,852,740,916 x 5

(4) 9,154,376,802 x 5

(5) 64,739 x 2

(6) 64,739 x 3

(7) 64,739 x 4

(8) 64,739 x 5

(9) 2,486,594,713 x 5

(10) 6,809,537,426 x 5

(11) 6,472,581,930 x 5

(12) 5,938,241,076 x 5

(13) 20,897 x 2

(14) 20,897 x 3

(15) 20,897 x 4

(16) 20,897 x 5

(17)
```
7,409,826,153
          x 5
-------------
```

(18)
```
  7,409,826,153
  7,409,826,153
  7,409,826,153
  7,409,826,153
+ 7,409,826,153
---------------
```

(19)
```
  2,153,064,978
  2,153,064,978
  2,153,064,978
  2,153,064,978
+ 2,153,064,978
---------------
```

(20)
```
2,153,064,978
          x 5
-------------
```

MASTERING THE MULTIPLICATION FACTS QUICKLY
FACILITY EXERCISES #11

Do the examples below.

(1) $\begin{array}{r} 4{,}372{,}095{,}168 \\ \times\ 6 \\ \hline \end{array}$

(2) $\begin{array}{r} 5{,}732{,}269{,}104 \\ \times\ 6 \\ \hline \end{array}$

(3) $\begin{array}{r} 7{,}018{,}329{,}546 \\ \times\ 6 \\ \hline \end{array}$

(4) $\begin{array}{r} 8{,}470{,}936{,}152 \\ \times\ 6 \\ \hline \end{array}$

(5) $\begin{array}{r} 8{,}476 \\ \times\ 2 \\ \hline \end{array}$

(6) $\begin{array}{r} 8{,}476 \\ \times\ 3 \\ \hline \end{array}$

(7) $\begin{array}{r} 8{,}476 \\ \times\ 4 \\ \hline \end{array}$

(8) $\begin{array}{r} 8{,}476 \\ \times\ 5 \\ \hline \end{array}$

(9) $\begin{array}{r} 8{,}476 \\ \times\ 6 \\ \hline \end{array}$

(10) $\begin{array}{r} 6{,}537{,}489{,}210 \\ \times\ 6 \\ \hline \end{array}$

(11) $\begin{array}{r} 1{,}785{,}049{,}623 \\ \times\ 6 \\ \hline \end{array}$

(12) $\begin{array}{r} 3{,}917{,}260{,}584 \\ \times\ 6 \\ \hline \end{array}$

(13) $\begin{array}{r} 2{,}589{,}302{,}476 \\ \times\ 6 \\ \hline \end{array}$

(14) $\begin{array}{r} 9{,}253 \\ \times\ 2 \\ \hline \end{array}$

(15) $\begin{array}{r} 9{,}253 \\ \times\ 3 \\ \hline \end{array}$

(16) $\begin{array}{r} 9{,}253 \\ \times\ 4 \\ \hline \end{array}$

(17)
```
 9,253
   x 5
------
```

(18)
```
 9,253
   x 6
------
```

(19)
```
  459,763
  459,763
  459,763
  459,763
  459,763
+ 459,763
---------
```

(20)
```
459,763
    x 6
-------
```

(21)
```
  78
  78
  78
  78
  78
+ 78
----
```

(22)
```
  78
 x 6
----
```

MASTERING THE MULTIPLICATION FACTS QUICKLY
FACILITY EXERCISES #12

Do the examples below.

(1) 1,493,265,087 x 6

(2) 6,483,504,791 x 6

(3) 3,852,740,916 x 6

(4) 9,154,376,802 x 6

(5) 2,486,594,713 x 6

(6) 6,809,537,425 x 6

(7) 76,498 x 2

(8) 76,498 x 3

(9) 76,498 x 4

(10) 76,498 x 5

(11) 76,498 x 6

(12) 6,472,581,930 x 6

(13) 5,938,241,076 x 6

(14) 1,069,547,283 x 6

(15) 1,498,625,307 x 6

(16)

2,846
2,846
2,846
2,846
2,846
+ 2,846

(17)

2,846
x 6

(18)

938
938
938
938
938
+ 938

(19)

938
x 6

MASTERING THE MULTIPLICATION FACTS QUICKLY
FACILITY EXERCISES #13

Do the examples below.

(1) 4,372,095,168 x 7

(2) 5,732,869,104 x 7

(3) 7,018,329,546 x 7

(4) 8,470,936,152 x 7

(5) 6,497 x 2

(6) 6,497 x 3

(7) 6,497 x 4

(8) 6,497 x 5

(9) 6,497 x 6

(10) 6,497 x 7

(11) 6,537,489,210 x 7

(12) 1,785,049,623 x 7

(13) 3,917,260,584 x 7

(14) 2,589,302,476 x 7

(15) 836 x 2

(16) 836 x 3

(17) 836 x 4

(18)
$$\begin{array}{r} 836 \\ \times\ 5 \\ \hline \end{array}$$

(19)
$$\begin{array}{r} 836 \\ \times\ 6 \\ \hline \end{array}$$

(20)
$$\begin{array}{r} 836 \\ \times\ 7 \\ \hline \end{array}$$

(21)
$$\begin{array}{r} 37{,}489 \\ 37{,}489 \\ 37{,}489 \\ 37{,}489 \\ 37{,}489 \\ 37{,}489 \\ +\ 37{,}489 \\ \hline \end{array}$$

(22)
$$\begin{array}{r} 37{,}489 \\ \times\ 7 \\ \hline \end{array}$$

(23)
$$\begin{array}{r} 698 \\ 698 \\ 698 \\ 698 \\ 698 \\ 698 \\ +\ 698 \\ \hline \end{array}$$

(24)
$$\begin{array}{r} 698 \\ \times\ 7 \\ \hline \end{array}$$

MASTERING THE MULTIPLICATION FACTS QUICKLY
FACILITY EXERCISES #14

Do the examples below.

(1) 1,493,265,087 x 7

(2) 6,483,504,791 x 7

(3) 3,852,740,916 x 7

(4) 9,154,376,802 x 7

(5) 584 x 2

(6) 584 x 3

(7) 584 x 4

(8) 584 x 5

(9) 584 x 6

(10) 584 x 7

(11) 2,486,594,713 x 7

(12) 6,809,537,425 x 7

(13) 6,472,581,930 x 7

(14) 7,264,805,318 x 7

(15) 965 x 2

(16) 965 x 3

(17) 965 x 4

(18)
```
  965
x   5
-----
```

(19)
```
  965
x   6
-----
```

(20)
```
  965
x   7
-----
```

(21)
```
   83,974
   83,974
   83,974
   83,974
   83,974
   83,974
+  83,974
---------
```

(22)
```
  83,974
x      7
--------
```

(23)
```
   749
   749
   749
   749
   749
   749
+  749
------
```

(24)
```
  749
x   7
-----
```

MASTERING THE MULTIPLICATION FACTS QUICKLY
FACILITY EXERCISES #15

Do the examples below.

(1) 1,493,265,087 x 8

(2) 6,483,504,791 x 8

(3) 3,852,740,916 x 8

(4) 9,154,376,802 x 8

(5) 674 x 2

(6) 674 x 3

(7) 674 x 4

(8) 674 x 5

(9) 674 x 6

(10) 674 x 7

(11) 674 x 8

(12) 2,486,594,713 x 8

(13) 6,809,537,425 x 8

(14) 6,472,581,930 x 8

(15) 7,264,805,318 x 8

(16) 396 x 2

(17) 396 x 3

(18) 396 x 4

(19) 396 x 5

(20) 396 x 6

(21) 396 x 7

(22) 396 x 8

(23)
6,795
6,795
6,795
6,795
6,795
6,795
6,795
+ 6,795

(24) 6,795 x 8

(25) 748 x 8

(26)
748
748
748
748
748
748
748
+ 748

MASTERING THE MULTIPLICATION FACTS QUICKLY
FACILITY EXERCISES #16

Do the examples below.

(1) 4,372,095,168 x 8

(2) 5,732,869,104 x 8

(3) 7,018,329,546 x 8

(4) 8,470,936,152 x 8

(5) 567 x 2

(6) 567 x 3

(7) 567 x 4

(8) 567 x 5

(9) 567 x 6

(10) 567 x 7

(11) 567 x 8

(12) 6,537,489,210 x 8

(13) 1,785,049,623 x 8

(14) 3,917,260,584 x 8

(15) 2,589,302,476 x 8

(16) 458 x 2

(17) 458 x 3

(18) 458 x 4

(19) 458
x 5

(20) 458
x 6

(21) 458
x 7

(22) 458
x 8

(23) 3,869
3,869
3,869
3,869
3,869
3,869
3,869
+ 3,869

(24) 3,869
x 8

(25) 754
x 8

(26) 754
754
754
754
754
754
754
+ 754

MASTERING THE MULTIPLICATION FACTS QUICKLY
FACILITY EXERCISES #17

Do the examples below.

(1) 2,589,302,476 x 9

(2) 3,917,260,584 x 9

(3) 1,785,049,623 x 9

(4) 6,537,489,210 x 9

(5) 987 x 2

(6) 987 x 3

(7) 987 x 4

(8) 987 x 5

(9) 987 x 6

(10) 987 x 7

(11) 987 x 8

(12) 987 x 9

(13) 8,470,936,152 x 9

(14) 7,018,329,546 x 9

(15) 5,732,869,104 x 9

(16) 4,372,095,168 x 9

(17) 847 x 2

(18) 847 x 3

(19) 847 x 4

(20) 847 x 5

(21) 847
x 6

(22) 847
x 7

(23) 847
x 8

(24) 847
x 9

(25) 76,984
76,984
76,984
76,984
76,984
76,984
76,984
76,984
+ 76,984

(26) 76,984
x 9

(27) 598
x 9

(28) 598
598
598
598
598
598
598
598
+ 598

MASTERING THE MULTIPLICATION FACTS QUICKLY
FACILITY EXERCISES #18

Do the examples below.

(1) 7,264,805,318 x 9

(2) 6,472,581,930 x 9

(3) 6,809,537,425 x 9

(4) 2,486,594,713 x 9

(5) 643 x 2

(6) 643 x 3

(7) 643 x 4

(8) 643 x 5

(9) 643 x 6

(10) 643 x 7

(11) 643 x 8

(12) 643 x 9

(13) 9,154,376,802 x 9

(14) 3,852,740,916 x 9

(15) 6,483,504,791 x 9

(16) 1,493,265,087 x 9

(17) 658 x 2

(18) 658 x 3

(19) 658 x 4

(20) 658 x 5

(21) 658
x 6

(22) 658
x 7

(23) 658
x 8

(24) 658
x 9

(25) 96,847
96,847
96,847
96,847
96,847
96,847
96,847
96,847
+ 96,847

(26) 96,847
x 9

(27) 498
x 9

(28) 498
498
498
498
498
498
498
498
+ 498

MASTERING THE MULTIPLICATION FACTS QUICKLY
FACILITY EXERCISES #19

Do the examples below.

(1) 4,568,097 x 2

(2) 4,568,097 x 3

(3) 4,568,097 x 4

(4) 4,568,097 x 5

(5) 4,568,097 x 6

(6) 4,568,097 x 7

(7) 4,568,097 x 8

(8) 4,568,097 x 9

(9) 4,568,097 x 10

(10) 5,182,763 x 6

(11) 5,182,763 x 7

(12) 5,182,763 x 8

(13) 5,182,763 x 9

(14) 5,182,763 x 10

(15) 5,182,763 x 1

MASTERING THE MULTIPLICATION FACTS QUICKLY
FACILITY EXERCISES #20

Do the examples below.

(1) 7,206,895 x 2	(2) 7,206,895 x 3	(3) 7,206,895 x 4
(4) 7,206,895 x 5	(5) 7,206,895 x 6	(6) 7,206,895 x 7
(7) 7,206,895 x 8	(8) 7,206,895 x 9	(9) 7,206,895 x 10
(10) 6,381,497 x 6	(11) 6,381,497 x 1	(12) 6,381,497 x 7
(13) 6,381,497 x 8	(14) 6,381,497 x 9	(15) 6,381,497 x 10

MASTERING THE MULTIPLICATION FACTS QUICKLY
FACILITY EXERCISES #21

Do the examples below.

(1) 2,489,673 x 2

(2) 2,489,673 x 3

(3) 2,489,673 x 4

(4) 2,489,673 x 5

(5) 2,489,673 x 6

(6) 2,489,673 x 7

(7) 705,982 x 6

(8) 705,982 x 7

(9) 705,982 x 8

(10) 695,400 x 9

(11) 7,386 x 6

(12) 96,348 x 8

(13) 3,526,242 x 8

(14) 3,526,242 x 9

(15) 3,526,242 x 10

(16)	(17)	(18)
$7 \times 3 =$ ____	$9 \times 5 =$ ____	$8 \times 6 =$ ____
$3\overline{)21}$	$5\overline{)45}$	$6 \times 8 =$ ____
$3 \times 7 =$ ____	$5 \times 9 =$ ____	$6\overline{)48}$
$7\overline{)21}$	$9\overline{)45}$	$8\overline{)48}$
(19)	**(20)**	**(21)**
$5 \times 3 =$ ____	$6 \times 5 =$ ____	$8 \times 4 =$ ____
$3\overline{)15}$	$5 \times 6 =$ ____	$8\overline{)32}$
$3 \times 5 =$ ____	$6\overline{)30}$	$4 \times 8 =$ ____
$5\overline{)15}$	$5\overline{)30}$	$4\overline{)32}$
(22)	**(23)**	**(24)**
$2 \times 10 =$ ____	$3 \times 10 =$ ____	$10 \times 7 =$ ____
$2\overline{)20}$	$10 \times 3 =$ ____	$7 \times 10 =$ ____
$10\overline{)20}$	$3\overline{)30}$	$7\overline{)70}$
$10 \times 2 =$ ____	$10\overline{)30}$	$10\overline{)70}$

(25)

$5 \times 10 =$ ____

$10 \times 5 =$ ____

$5 \overline{)\,50}$

$10 \overline{)\,50}$

(26)

$10 \times 9 =$ ____

$9 \overline{)\,90}$

$9 \times 10 =$ ____

$10 \overline{)\,90}$

(27)

$10 \times 6 =$ ____

$10 \overline{)\,60}$

$6 \overline{)\,60}$

$6 \times 10 =$ ____

LINKING MULTIPLICATION AND DIVISION FACTS
FACILITY EXERCISES #23

Say the question each example asks and write your answer in the space provided.

(1)	(2)	(3)
$4 \times \underline{\quad\quad} = 20$	$3 \times \underline{\quad\quad} = 27$	$\underline{\quad\quad} \times 9 = 18$
$6 \times \underline{\quad\quad} = 18$	$\underline{\quad\quad} \times 8 = 32$	$\underline{\quad\quad} \times 2 = 4$
$\underline{\quad\quad} \times 4 = 8$	$4 \times \underline{\quad\quad} = 32$	$7 \times \underline{\quad\quad} = 49$
$7 \times \underline{\quad\quad} = 21$	$5 \times \underline{\quad\quad} = 30$	$5 \times \underline{\quad\quad} = 35$
(4)	**(5)**	**(6)**
$\underline{\quad\quad} \times 5 = 15$	$5 \times \underline{\quad\quad} = 10$	$2 \times \underline{\quad\quad} = 6$
$8 \times \underline{\quad\quad} = 8$	$\underline{\quad\quad} \times 10 = 70$	$7 \times \underline{\quad\quad} = 42$
$\underline{\quad\quad} \times 5 = 10$	$3 \times \underline{\quad\quad} = 9$	$\underline{\quad\quad} \times 2 = 12$
$\underline{\quad\quad} \times 8 = 48$	$\underline{\quad\quad} \times 4 = 4$	$7 \times \underline{\quad\quad} = 14$
(7)	**(8)**	**(9)**
$8 \times \underline{\quad\quad} = 24$	$9 \times \underline{\quad\quad} = 36$	$\underline{\quad\quad} \times 7 = 7$
$\underline{\quad\quad} \times 4 = 12$	$\underline{\quad\quad} \times 5 = 25$	$9 \times \underline{\quad\quad} = 81$
$4 \times \underline{\quad\quad} = 24$	$8 \times \underline{\quad\quad} = 64$	$\underline{\quad\quad} \times 9 = 72$
$3 \times \underline{\quad\quad} = 18$	$7 \times \underline{\quad\quad} = 63$	$10 \times \underline{\quad\quad} = 60$

(10)

$8 \times \underline{\qquad} = 56$

$\underline{\qquad} \times 4 = 16$

$6 \times \underline{\qquad} = 6$

$\underline{\qquad} \times 7 = 49$

(11)

$10 \times \underline{\qquad} = 50$

$7 \times \underline{\qquad} = 28$

$2 \times \underline{\qquad} = 16$

$5 \times \underline{\qquad} = 45$

(12)

$\underline{\qquad} \times 9 = 54$

$6 \times \underline{\qquad} = 36$

$\underline{\qquad} \times 5 = 40$

$\underline{\qquad} \times 4 = 40$

(13)

$2 \times \underline{\qquad} = 12$

$8 \times \underline{\qquad} = 16$

$\underline{\qquad} \times 2 = 18$

$\underline{\qquad} \times 1 = 3$

(14)

$\underline{\qquad} \times 3 = 6$

$12 \times \underline{\qquad} = 12$

$9 \times \underline{\qquad} = 9$

$\underline{\qquad} \times 6 = 12$

(15)

$3 \times \underline{\qquad} = 12$

$10 \times \underline{\qquad} = 30$

$\underline{\qquad} \times 3 = 30$

$3 \times \underline{\qquad} = 21$

(16)

$\underline{\qquad} \times 3 = 15$

$1 \times \underline{\qquad} = 4$

$10 \times \underline{\qquad} = 90$

$\underline{\qquad} \times 3 = 24$

(17)

$6 \times \underline{\qquad} = 48$

$\underline{\qquad} \times 4 = 28$

$4 \times \underline{\qquad} = 36$

$10 \times \underline{\qquad} = 80$

(18)

$6 \times \underline{\qquad} = 30$

$\underline{\qquad} \times 7 = 35$

$6 \times \underline{\qquad} = 42$

$7 \times \underline{\qquad} = 56$

LINKING MULTIPLICATION AND DIVISION FACTS
FACILITY EXERCISES #24

Write your answers on top of the examples.

(1)	(2)	(3)	(4)
$5\overline{)30}$	$6\overline{)30}$	$3\overline{)27}$	$8\overline{)32}$
(5)	(6)	(7)	(8)
$4\overline{)32}$	$5\overline{)35}$	$7\overline{)35}$	$7\overline{)49}$
(9)	(10)	(11)	(12)
$2\overline{)6}$	$9\overline{)18}$	$7\overline{)21}$	$3\overline{)21}$
(13)	(14)	(15)	(16)
$4\overline{)4}$	$6\overline{)18}$	$5\overline{)20}$	$7\overline{)7}$
(17)	(18)	(19)	(20)
$1\overline{)7}$	$8\overline{)64}$	$5\overline{)25}$	$9\overline{)9}$
(21)	(22)	(23)	(24)
$1\overline{)9}$	$7\overline{)63}$	$2\overline{)12}$	$7\overline{)14}$

(25)	(26)	(27)	(28)
$8\overline{)56}$	$5\overline{)15}$	$6\overline{)36}$	$8\overline{)72}$
(29)	**(30)**	**(31)**	**(32)**
$2\overline{)10}$	$3\overline{)24}$	$7\overline{)42}$	$9\overline{)81}$
(33)	**(34)**	**(35)**	**(36)**
$10\overline{)20}$	$10\overline{)30}$	$10\overline{)40}$	$10\overline{)50}$
(37)	**(38)**	**(39)**	**(40)**
$10\overline{)60}$	$10\overline{)70}$	$10\overline{)80}$	$10\overline{)90}$
(41)	**(42)**	**(43)**	**(44)**
$2\overline{)4}$	$3\overline{)9}$	$4\overline{)12}$	$5\overline{)40}$
(45)	**(46)**	**(47)**	**(48)**
$6\overline{)48}$	$7\overline{)28}$	$8\overline{)80}$	$6\overline{)60}$
(49)	**(50)**	**(51)**	**(52)**
$6\overline{)6}$	$9\overline{)72}$	$4\overline{)16}$	$8\overline{)24}$

PREPARING FOR DIVISION WITH REMAINDER
FACILITY EXERCISES #25

Write the answers in the spaces provided. Be sure to multiply before you add.

(1)	(2)	(3)
$6 \times 9 + 3 =$ ____	$9 \times 5 + 4 =$ ____	$5 \times 4 +$ ____ $= 23$
$8 \times 4 + 2 =$ ____	$2 \times 3 + 1 =$ ____	$7 \times 3 +$ ____ $= 22$
$2 \times 9 + 1 =$ ____	$3 \times 5 + 2 =$ ____	$4 \times 4 +$ ____ $= 19$

(4)	(5)	(6)
$10 \times 7 + 6 =$ ____	$2 \times$ ____ $+ 3 = 13$	$7 \times 7 +$ ____ $= 55$
$10 \times 8 + 7 =$ ____	$7 \times$ ____ $+ 5 = 47$	$3 \times 3 +$ ____ $= 11$
$6 \times 3 + 2 =$ ____	$8 \times$ ____ $+ 5 = 69$	$5 \times 5 +$ ____ $= 28$

(7)	(8)	(9)
$4 \times 9 +$ ____ $= 39$	$5 \times$ ____ $+ 1 = 51$	$4 \times$ ____ $+ 2 = 30$
$6 \times 6 +$ ____ $= 41$	$9 \times$ ____ $+ 6 = 78$	$2 \times 2 + 1 =$ ____
$3 \times 8 +$ ____ $= 26$	$6 \times$ ____ $+ 1 = 25$	$2 \times$ ____ $+ 6 = 26$

(10)	(11)	(12)
$2 \times 7 +$ ____ $= 17$	$6 \times 1 +$ ____ $= 10$	$7 \times 8 +$ ____ $= 62$
$8 \times$ ____ $+ 9 = 89$	$6 \times$ ____ $+ 7 = 61$	$9 \times 2 +$ ____ $= 19$
$7 \times$ ____ $+ 5 = 12$	$5 \times 6 +$ ____ $= 34$	$3 \times$ ____ $+ 3 = 15$

(13)

$4 \times \_\_\_\_ + 3 = 23$

$3 \times 9 + \_\_\_\_ = 29$

$6 \times \_\_\_\_ + 3 = 21$

(14)

$5 \times 8 + \_\_\_\_ = 44$

$4 \times \_\_\_\_ + 1 = 9$

$5 \times 2 + \_\_\_\_ = 11$

(15)

$9 \times \_\_\_\_ + 8 = 89$

$5 \times \_\_\_\_ + 8 = 43$

$2 \times 6 + \_\_\_\_ = 17$

---

(16)

$5 \times 1 + \_\_\_\_ = 8$

$4 \times 3 + \_\_\_\_ = 15$

$7 \times \_\_\_\_ + 5 = 19$

(17)

$5 \times 4 + 4 = \_\_\_\_$

$2 \times \_\_\_\_ + 1 = 3$

$3 \times 2 + 1 = \_\_\_\_$

(18)

$6 \times \_\_\_\_ + 3 = 33$

$8 \times 2 + 6 = \_\_\_\_$

$4 \times 1 + \_\_\_\_ = 7$

---

(19)

$8 \times 5 + \_\_\_\_ = 47$

$9 \times \_\_\_\_ + 8 = 71$

(20)

$7 \times 8 + \_\_\_\_ = 60$

$3 \times 7 + 5 = \_\_\_\_$

(21)

$6 \times 6 + \_\_\_\_ = 41$

$8 \times 8 + \_\_\_\_ = 70$

SHORT DIVISION WITH REMAINDER
FACILITY EXERCISES #26

Write your answers on top of the examples. On extra sheets of paper, you should also do most of these problems by repeated subtractions.

(1)

$4\overline{)15}$

Check

(2)

$4\overline{)18}$

Check

(3)

$5\overline{)12}$

Check

(4)

$7\overline{)20}$

Check

(5)

$2\overline{)13}$

Check

(6)

$7\overline{)8}$

Check

(7)

$6\overline{)9}$

Check

(8)

$8\overline{)17}$

Check

(9)

$7\overline{)32}$

Check

(10)

$2\overline{)3}$

Check

(11)

$5\overline{)24}$

Check

(12)

$7\overline{)18}$

Check

(13)

$6\overline{)17}$

Check

(14)

$9\overline{)38}$

Check

(15)

$3\overline{)10}$

Check

(16)

$8\overline{)21}$

Check

(17) $4\overline{)33}$ **Check**

(18) $6\overline{)45}$ **Check**

(19) $7\overline{)40}$ **Check**

(20) $3\overline{)13}$ **Check**

(21) $5\overline{)39}$ **Check**

(22) $9\overline{)20}$ **Check**

(23) $2\overline{)17}$ **Check**

(24) $5\overline{)52}$ **Check**

(25) $9\overline{)56}$ **Check**

(26) $8\overline{)37}$ **Check**

(27) $7\overline{)45}$ **Check**

(28) $7\overline{)60}$ **Check**

(29) $8\overline{)43}$ **Check**

(30) $7\overline{)58}$ **Check**

(31) $10\overline{)68}$ **Check**

(32) $8\overline{)13}$ **Check**

(33)

$6\overline{)27}$

Check

(34)

$4\overline{)39}$

Check

(35)

$3\overline{)28}$

Check

(36)

$8\overline{)75}$

Check

(37)

$9\overline{)84}$

Check

(38)

$4\overline{)27}$

Check

(39)

$8\overline{)63}$

Check

(40)

$7\overline{)55}$

Check

(41)

$9\overline{)16}$

Check

(42)

$7\overline{)30}$

Check

(43)

$4\overline{)30}$

Check

(44)

$9\overline{)30}$

Check

(45)

$6\overline{)44}$

Check

(46)

$5\overline{)44}$

Check

(47)

$5\overline{)16}$

Check

(48)

$7\overline{)56}$

Check

(49)	(50)	(51)	(52)
$6\overline{)56}$ Check	$9\overline{)56}$ Check	$5\overline{)19}$ Check	$2\overline{)9}$ Check
(53)	(54)	(55)	(56)
$8\overline{)19}$ Check	$8\overline{)73}$ Check	$9\overline{)73}$ Check	$7\overline{)50}$ Check
(57)	(58)	(59)	(60)
$6\overline{)51}$ Check	$8\overline{)51}$ Check	$7\overline{)16}$ Check	$7\overline{)67}$ Check
(61)	(62)	(63)	(64)
$9\overline{)67}$ Check	$8\overline{)67}$ Check	$7\overline{)13}$ Check	$9\overline{)13}$ Check

FACILITY EXERCISES #27
Mixed Practice

Write your answers in the space provided.

1. Find answers to the examples below without use of fingers.

(a) **8 + 9 – 6 – 4 + 7 + 5 – 3 =_______**

(b) **15 + 8 – 6 + 4 – 8 – 4 + 9 =_______**

2. Do each addition and subtraction below. Check the answer to each subtraction.

(a)
$$\begin{array}{r} 695{,}000{,}827 \\ -\ \underline{596{,}704{,}947} \end{array}$$

(b)
$$\begin{array}{r} 2{,}795{,}846 \\ +\ \underline{7{,}615{,}842} \end{array}$$

3. Start at zero and count by eights to eighty.

4. Start at six and count by sevens to seventy-six.

5. Start at fifty-three and count backwards by fives to three.

6. Start at seventy-two and count backwards by seven to two.

7. Read each numeral below:

(a) **498,000,498,000,498**

(b) **100,100,100,100,100**

(c) **10,000,000,000**

8. Name the number which each digit in 207,083,690,000 represents.

9. Name the value of each place in 7,083,690,000.

10. The number 7,083,690,200 is in
- **(a)** which ones? ______
- **(b)** which billions? ______
- **(c)** which tens? ______
- **(d)** which hundred-millions? ______
- **(e)** which hundred-thousands? ______
- **(f)** which ten-millions? ______
- **(g)** which thousands? ______
- **(h)** which millions? ______
- **(i)** which ten-thousands? ______
- **(j)** which hundreds? ______

11. Tell the truth as you do the addition and subtraction below.

(a) $\begin{array}{r} 950{,}749 \\ +\ 879{,}605 \\ \hline \end{array}$

(b) $\begin{array}{r} 6{,}753{,}005 \\ -\ 6{,}597{,}063 \\ \hline \end{array}$

12. Find the missing numbers.

(a) 105 = 47 + ______

(b) 201 − ______ = 79

(c) 273 = ______ − 486

(d) ______ + 23 = 81

13. Add the following:

$\begin{array}{r} 5{,}479 \\ 2{,}865 \\ 3{,}978 \\ 9{,}467 \\ 7{,}857 \\ 6{,}984 \\ 4{,}789 \\ 6{,}956 \\ 8{,}888 \\ 9{,}999 \\ 7{,}777 \\ +\ 6{,}548 \\ \hline \end{array}$

14. Do the following multiplications:

(a) $\begin{array}{r} 498{,}037 \\ \text{x } 6 \\ \hline \end{array}$

(b) $\begin{array}{r} 748{,}695 \\ \text{x } 9 \\ \hline \end{array}$

(c) $\begin{array}{r} 604{,}783 \\ \text{x } 7 \\ \hline \end{array}$

15. Do the following divisions:

(a) $4\overline{)\,28}$

(b) $7\overline{)\,60}$

(c) $8\overline{)\,51}$

MORE MULTIPLICATION FACTS
FACILITY EXERCISES #28

Do each example by the method of counting zeros. Write answers in the spaces provided.

1. **100 x 100 =** ________________
2. **10 x 100,000 =** ________________
3. **1,000 x 1,000 =** ________________
4. **10,000 x 1,000 =** ________________
5. **10 x 10 =** ________________
6. **100 x 1,000,000 =** ________________
7. **1,000 x 1,000 =** ________________
8. **100,000 x 1,000 =** ________________
9. **100 x 10 =** ________________
10. **10,000 x 100 =** ________________
11. **1,000,000 x 10,000 =** ________________
12. **10 x 1,000 =** ________________
13. **700 x 1,000 =** ________________
14. **9 x 100,000 =** ________________
15. **10 x 8 =** ________________
16. **500 x 10,000 =** ________________
17. **1,000,000 x 30 =** ________________
18. **1,000 x 2,000 =** ________________
19. **50,000 x 1,000 =** ________________
20. **100,000 x 700 =** ________________
21. **800,000 x 10,000 =** ________________
22. **9,000 x 10 =** ________________
23. **3,000,000 x 1,000 =** ________________
24. **5 x 100 =** ________________
25. **100,000 x 7 =** ________________
26. **20 x 10 =** ________________
27. **4,000 x 10,000,000 =** ________________
28. **10 x 700 =** ________________
29. **1,000 x 8 =** ________________
30. **60,000 x 100 =** ________________
31. **80 x 100 =** ________________
32. **10,000 x 4,000 =** ________________
33. **700,000 x 10,000 =** ________________

PREPARING FOR MULTIPLICATION BY TWO OR MORE DIGITS
FACILITY EXERCISES #29

Expand each product.

(1)

983 x 10 = __________ + __________ + __________

640 x 100 = __________ + __________

89 x 1,000 = __________ + __________

(2)

318 x 42 = __________ + __________ + __________

42 x 318 = __________ + __________

508 x 67 = __________ + __________

(3)

306 x 873 = __________ + __________

750 x 10 = __________ + __________

333 x 1,000 = __________ + __________ + __________

(4)

44 x 444 = __________ + __________

414 x 44 = __________ + __________ + __________

356 x 783 = __________ + __________ + __________

(5)

17 x 529 = __________ + __________

960 x 75 = __________ + __________

75 x 111 = __________ + __________

(6)

320 x 510 = ________________ + ________________

209 x 638 = ________________ + ________________

12 x 702 = ________________ + ________________

(7)

432 x 668 = ________________ + ________________ + ________________

23 x 10 = ________________ + ________________

(8)

83 x 10 = ________________ + ________________

19 x 537 = ________________ + ________________

537 x 19 = ________________ + ________________ + ________________

(9)

67 x 100 = ________________ + ________________

437 x 186 = ________________ + ________________ + ________________

186 x 437 = ________________ + ________________ + ________________

(10)

4,763 x 809 = ____________ + ____________ + ____________ + ____________

809 x 4,763 = ________________ + ________________

2,070 x 4,001 = ________________ + ________________

(11)

801,070 x 670 = ________________ + ________________ + ________________

670 x 801,070 = ________________ + ________________

PREPARING FOR MULTIPLICATION BY TWO OR MORE DIGITS
FACILITY EXERCISES #30

Do each example by the method of counting zeros. Write answers in the spaces provided.

(1)

384 x 10 = ________

57 x 10,000 = ________

100 x 1,538 = ________

7,601 x 1,000 = ________

(2)

384 x 1,000 = ________

1,538 x 1,000 = ________

10 x 1,538 = ________

398 x 100 = ________

(3)

450 x 100 = ________

100,000 x 50 = ________

8,730 x 10 = ________

10,000 x 100 = ________

(4)

27,000 x 100 = ________

800 x 10,000 = ________

100 x 8,700 = ________

100 x 1,000 = ________

(5)

3,008 x 1,000 = ________

8 x 100,000 = ________

(6)

370 x 1,000 = ________

504 x 10 = ________

PREPARING FOR MULTIPLICATION BY TWO OR MORE DIGITS
FACILITY EXERCISES #31

Write answers in the spaces provided.

(1)

4 x 8 = ____________________

4 x 80 = ____________________

4 x 800 = ____________________

4 x 8,000 = ____________________

4 x 8,000,000 = ____________

(2)

40 x 8 = ____________________

400 x 8 = ____________________

4,000 x 8 = ________________

400,000 x 8 = ______________

4,000,000 x 8 = ____________

(3)

40 x 80 = ____________________

4,000 x 80 = ________________

400 x 800 = ________________

4,000 x 80,000 = ____________

400 x 8,000 = ______________

(4)

600 x 90 = ____________________

2 x 7,000,000 = ______________

3,000 x 3,000 = ______________

7,000,000 x 800 = ____________

60,000,000 x 4,000 = __________

(5)

5 x 6 = ____________________

5 x 60 = ____________________

50 x 6 = ____________________

50 x 60 = ____________________

500 x 60 = ____________________

(6)

5 x 4,000 = ____________________

50 x 4,000 = ________________

5,000 x 4,000 = ______________

500 x 400 = ________________

5,000,000 x 40,000 = __________

(7)

800 x 5,000 = ______________

2,000 x 50 = ______________

90,000 x 500 = ______________

700 x 50,000 = ______________

6,000 x 4,000 = ____________

(8)

70 x 3,000 = ________________

600 x 30 = ____________________

80,000 x 9,000 = ____________

40,000 x 40,000 = ____________

30 x 900 = ____________________

PREPARING FOR MULTIPLICATION BY TWO OR MORE DIGITS
FACILITY EXERCISES #32

Complete the following statements:

1. **Seventy hundreds = Seven ______________________________**

2. **Ninety ten-thousands = Nine ______________________________**

3. **Twenty millions = Two ______________________________**

4. **Thirty ones = Three ______________________________**

5. **Sixty hundred-millions = Six ______________________________**

6. **Forty hundred-billions = Four ______________________________**

7. **Eighty trillions = Eight ______________________________**

8. **Ten hundreds = One ______________________________**

9. **Fifty ten-millions = Five ______________________________**

10. **Ninety ten-trillions = Nine ______________________________**

11. **Seventy hundred-thousands = Seven ______________________________**

12. **Ten ten-billions = One ______________________________**

13. **Forty thousands = Four ______________________________**

14. **Ten hundred-millions = One ______________________________**

15. **Eighty billions = Eight ______________________________**

TELLING THE TRUTH WHEN MULTIPLYING WHOLE NUMBERS
FACILITY EXERCISES #33

Do the following multiplication examples by telling the truth.

(1) 3,750,185,924 × 2

(2) 3,750,185,924 × 3

(3) 3,750,185,924 × 4

(4) 3,750,185,924 × 5

(5) 3,750,185,924 × 6

(6) 3,750,185,924 × 7

(7) 3,750,185,924 × 8

(8) 3,750,185,924 × 9

(9) 3,750,185,924 × 10

(10) 6,139,402,785 × 2

(11) 8,429,507,913 × 3

(12) 4,028,195,367 × 4

(13) 8,479,513,460 × 8

(14) 7,053,294,861 × 6

(15) 2,138,049,675 × 7

(16) $\begin{array}{r} 1{,}390{,}468{,}527 \\ \times\ 5 \\ \hline \end{array}$

(17) $\begin{array}{r} 9{,}584{,}736{,}201 \\ \times\ 9 \\ \hline \end{array}$

(18) $\begin{array}{r} 5{,}428{,}479{,}360 \\ \times\ 8 \\ \hline \end{array}$

(19) $\begin{array}{r} 4{,}705{,}891{,}423 \\ \times\ 6 \\ \hline \end{array}$

(20) $\begin{array}{r} 6{,}954{,}072{,}831 \\ \times\ 7 \\ \hline \end{array}$

(21) $\begin{array}{r} 4{,}738{,}409{,}152 \\ \times\ 9 \\ \hline \end{array}$

(22) $\begin{array}{r} 9{,}876{,}543{,}210 \\ \times\ 4 \\ \hline \end{array}$

(23) $\begin{array}{r} 9{,}081{,}736{,}452 \\ \times\ 3 \\ \hline \end{array}$

(24) $\begin{array}{r} 4{,}837{,}598{,}206 \\ \times\ 8 \\ \hline \end{array}$

(25) $\begin{array}{r} 2{,}641{,}073{,}894 \\ \times\ 7 \\ \hline \end{array}$

(26) $\begin{array}{r} 6{,}058{,}147{,}293 \\ \times\ 5 \\ \hline \end{array}$

TELLING THE TRUTH WHEN MULTIPLYING WHOLE NUMBERS
FACILITY EXERCISES #34

Do each multiplication below using the short-cut method in two ways: by telling the truth and without telling the truth (no reference to place value).

(1) 453×46

(2) 729×58

(3) $3{,}849 \times 27$

(4) 968×14

(5) $7{,}962 \times 34$

(6) 287×63

(7) 594×96

(8) 645×86

(9) 846×95

(10) $2{,}637 \times 72$

(11) 704×68

(12) 806×45

(13) 890×28

(14) 320×49

(15) $8{,}276 \times 94$

(16) 417×78

(17) $1{,}256 \times 89$

(18) 908×65

(19) 370×25

(20) 419×16

(21) $\begin{array}{r} 673 \\ \times 13 \\ \hline \end{array}$

(22) $\begin{array}{r} 7,424 \\ \times 18 \\ \hline \end{array}$

(23) $\begin{array}{r} 9,547 \\ \times 23 \\ \hline \end{array}$

(24) $\begin{array}{r} 212 \\ \times 31 \\ \hline \end{array}$

(25) $\begin{array}{r} 485 \\ \times 17 \\ \hline \end{array}$

(26) $\begin{array}{r} 485 \\ \times 71 \\ \hline \end{array}$

(27) $\begin{array}{r} 608 \\ \times 59 \\ \hline \end{array}$

(28) $\begin{array}{r} 608 \\ \times 12 \\ \hline \end{array}$

(29) $\begin{array}{r} 345 \\ \times 84 \\ \hline \end{array}$

(30) $\begin{array}{r} 1,274 \\ \times 67 \\ \hline \end{array}$

(31) $\begin{array}{r} 285 \\ \times 93 \\ \hline \end{array}$

(32) $\begin{array}{r} 6,428 \\ \times 15 \\ \hline \end{array}$

(33) $\begin{array}{r} 7,890 \\ \times 36 \\ \hline \end{array}$

(34) $\begin{array}{r} 8,460 \\ \times 70 \\ \hline \end{array}$

(35) $\begin{array}{r} 600 \\ \times 49 \\ \hline \end{array}$

(36) $\begin{array}{r} 800 \\ \times 50 \\ \hline \end{array}$

(37) Expand **47 x 693** as a sum of six partial products:

________ + ________ + ________ + ________ + ________ + ________

(38) Expand **68 x 47** as a sum of four partial products:

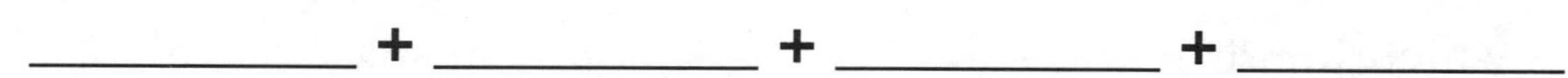

FACILITY EXERCISES #35
Mixed Practice

Write your answers in the spaces provided.

1. Find the answers to the examples below without use of fingers.

(a) **9 + 4 + 8 – 10 – 5 – 6 = _______**

(b) **27 – 8 – 7 – 6 + 5 + 9 – 3 – 4 – 5 + 2 = _______**

2. Do the addition and subtraction below. Check the answer to the subtraction.

(a)
$$\begin{array}{r} 43,857,059 \\ +\ 89,562,986 \\ \hline \end{array}$$

(b)
$$\begin{array}{r} 800,500,093 \\ -\ 786,317,895 \\ \hline \end{array}$$

3. Start at zero and count by nines to ninety.

4. Start at two and count by eights to eighty-two.

5. Start at seventy-four and count backward by sevens to four.

6. Read each numeral below:

(a) **111,000,000,000,111**
(b) **100,001,010,100,001**
(c) **100,000,000**

7. Name the value of each digit in 666,666,666,666.

8. Name the value of each place in 666,666,666,666.

9. The number 483,752 is in

(a) which tens? ____________________

(b) which thousands? ____________________

(c) which ones? ____________________

(d) which ten thousands? ____________________

(e) which hundreds? ____________________

(f) which hundred-thousands? ____________________

10. Tell the truth as you do the addition and subtraction example below.

(a) $\begin{array}{r} 8{,}570{,}937 \\ +\ 6{,}090{,}938 \\ \hline \end{array}$

(b) $\begin{array}{r} 8{,}570{,}937 \\ -\ 6{,}090{,}938 \\ \hline \end{array}$

11. Find the missing numbers.

(a) ______ + 69 = 240

(b) ______ – 427 = 183

(c) 293 = 609 – ______

(d) 525 = 428 + ______

12. Add the following:

$\begin{array}{r} 63{,}497 \\ 8{,}768 \\ 875 \\ 49{,}597 \\ 86 \\ 57{,}769 \\ 985 \\ 7 \\ 868 \\ 98{,}699 \\ 756 \\ 97 \\ 6{,}985 \\ 89{,}578 \\ +\ 869 \\ \hline \end{array}$

13. Do the following divisions:

(a) $5\overline{)44}$ (b) $9\overline{)63}$ (c) $7\overline{)47}$

14. Do the following multiplications:

(a) 83 x 10,000 = ________

(b) 64 x 7,000 = ________

(c) 291 x 100 = ________

15. Expand **58 x 94** as a sum of four partial products:

______ + ______ + ______ + ______

16. Expand **62 x 478** as a sum of six partial products:

______ + ______ + ______ + ______ + ______ + ______

17. Do the following multiplications:

(a) $\begin{array}{r} 709 \\ \times\ 34 \\ \hline \end{array}$

(b) $\begin{array}{r} 846 \\ \times\ 78 \\ \hline \end{array}$

(c) $\begin{array}{r} 397 \\ \times\ 96 \\ \hline \end{array}$

TELLING THE TRUTH WHEN MULTIPLYING WHOLE NUMBERS
FACILITY EXERCISES #36

Do the multiplications below by the short-cut method and without telling the truth (no reference to place value).

(1) $\begin{array}{r} 438 \\ \times\ 276 \\ \hline \end{array}$

(2) $\begin{array}{r} 874 \\ \times\ 342 \\ \hline \end{array}$

(3) $\begin{array}{r} 593 \\ \times\ 685 \\ \hline \end{array}$

(4) $\begin{array}{r} 914 \\ \times\ 681 \\ \hline \end{array}$

(5) $\begin{array}{r} 647 \\ \times\ 647 \\ \hline \end{array}$

(6) $\begin{array}{r} 184 \\ \times\ 480 \\ \hline \end{array}$

(7) $\begin{array}{r} 3{,}796 \\ \times\ 478 \\ \hline \end{array}$

(8) $\begin{array}{r} 408 \\ \times\ 804 \\ \hline \end{array}$

(9) $\begin{array}{r} 810 \\ \times\ 674 \\ \hline \end{array}$

(10) $\begin{array}{r} 717 \\ \times\ 216 \\ \hline \end{array}$

(11) $\begin{array}{r} 694 \\ \times\ 700 \\ \hline \end{array}$

(12) $\begin{array}{r} 724 \\ \times\ 60 \\ \hline \end{array}$

(13) $\begin{array}{r} 7{,}648 \\ \times\ 782 \\ \hline \end{array}$

(14) $\begin{array}{r} 5{,}009 \\ \times\ 37 \\ \hline \end{array}$

(15) $\begin{array}{r} 947 \\ \times\ 860 \\ \hline \end{array}$

(16) $\begin{array}{r} 385 \\ \times\ 903 \\ \hline \end{array}$

(17) $\begin{array}{r} 6{,}794 \\ \times\ 87 \\ \hline \end{array}$

(18) $\begin{array}{r} 3{,}981 \\ \times\ 400 \\ \hline \end{array}$

(19) $\begin{array}{r} 47 \\ \times\ 346 \\ \hline \end{array}$

(20) $\begin{array}{r} 209 \\ \times\ 704 \\ \hline \end{array}$

(21) $\begin{array}{r} 800 \\ \times\ 647 \\ \hline \end{array}$	(22) $\begin{array}{r} 679 \\ \times\ 679 \\ \hline \end{array}$	(23) $\begin{array}{r} 348 \\ \times\ 6{,}583 \\ \hline \end{array}$	(24) $\begin{array}{r} 600 \\ \times\ 500 \\ \hline \end{array}$
(25) $\begin{array}{r} 47 \\ \times\ 62 \\ \hline \end{array}$	(26) $\begin{array}{r} 400 \\ \times\ 7{,}469 \\ \hline \end{array}$	(27) $\begin{array}{r} 7{,}469 \\ \times\ 400 \\ \hline \end{array}$	(28) $\begin{array}{r} 537 \\ \times\ 693 \\ \hline \end{array}$
(29) $\begin{array}{r} 693 \\ \times\ 537 \\ \hline \end{array}$	(30) $\begin{array}{r} 726 \\ \times\ 3{,}475 \\ \hline \end{array}$	(31) $\begin{array}{r} 3{,}475 \\ \times\ 726 \\ \hline \end{array}$	(32) $\begin{array}{r} 108 \\ \times\ 205 \\ \hline \end{array}$
(33) $\begin{array}{r} 6{,}007 \\ \times\ 7{,}006 \\ \hline \end{array}$	(34) $\begin{array}{r} 8{,}796 \\ \times\ 570 \\ \hline \end{array}$	(35) $\begin{array}{r} 570 \\ \times\ 8{,}796 \\ \hline \end{array}$	(36) $\begin{array}{r} 490 \\ \times\ 830 \\ \hline \end{array}$
(37) $\begin{array}{r} 4{,}683 \\ \times\ 920 \\ \hline \end{array}$	(38) $\begin{array}{r} 920 \\ \times\ 4{,}684 \\ \hline \end{array}$	(39) $\begin{array}{r} 143 \\ \times\ 143 \\ \hline \end{array}$	(40) $\begin{array}{r} 294 \\ \times\ 429 \\ \hline \end{array}$

(41) $\begin{array}{r} 314 \\ \times\ 612 \\ \hline \end{array}$

(42) $\begin{array}{r} 612 \\ \times\ 314 \\ \hline \end{array}$

(43) $\begin{array}{r} 703 \\ \times\ 730 \\ \hline \end{array}$

(44) $\begin{array}{r} 647 \\ \times\ 480 \\ \hline \end{array}$

(45) $\begin{array}{r} 480 \\ \times\ 647 \\ \hline \end{array}$

(46) $\begin{array}{r} 670 \\ \times\ 509 \\ \hline \end{array}$

(47) $\begin{array}{r} 328 \\ \times\ 900 \\ \hline \end{array}$

(48) $\begin{array}{r} 8,000 \\ \times\ 5,000 \\ \hline \end{array}$

(49) $\begin{array}{r} 83,486 \\ \times\ 75 \\ \hline \end{array}$

(50) $\begin{array}{r} 60,985 \\ \times\ 6 \\ \hline \end{array}$

(51) $\begin{array}{r} 34,162 \\ \times\ 47 \\ \hline \end{array}$

(52) $\begin{array}{r} 58,429 \\ \times\ 84 \\ \hline \end{array}$

(53) $\begin{array}{r} 79,587 \\ \times\ 8 \\ \hline \end{array}$

(54) $\begin{array}{r} 89,674 \\ \times\ 96 \\ \hline \end{array}$

SOLVING WORD PROBLEMS
FACILITY EXERCISES #37

Do the word problems below.

1. If one lamp costs $86, what is the cost of 10,000 of those lamps?

2. Find the cost of 58 sofas if each one of them costs $759.

3. How much money will Mr. Hall need to buy 324 coats for his store if each one costs $97?

4. How much money will Miss Santiago need to buy 27 games at $23 each and 34 toys at $26 each?

5. How much money will you need to buy 75 chairs at $32 each and 18 tables at $72 each?

6. How much will it cost to buy 1,000 calculators at $27 each and 100 watches at $235 each?

7. If you have $38,000, can you buy 100 TV sets at $475 each?

8. If you have $3,675, can you buy 10 cameras at $245 each? Can you buy 20 of these cameras?

9. If Sally has $115 and buys 10 dolls at $8 each, how much money does she have left?

10. If you have $68 and you buy 4 toys at $9 each, how much money do you have left? What is the largest number of these toys you can buy? Will you have any money left over after buying the maximum number of toys?

11. How many books are in 46 boxes if each contains 30 books?

12. If you receive 100 boxes with 25 books in each and 80 boxes with 30 books in each, how many books did you get?

13. If Mr. Stern has $257,500 and he buys 3,000 lamps at $43 each, how much money does he have left? Could he buy 8,000 lamps? What is the maximum thousands of lamps he could buy?

14. How much will it cost to buy 5 pens at $4 each; 6 notebooks at $3 each; 2 bottles of glue at $2 each; and 3 bookbags at $5 each?

When you have finished these problems, return to Facility Exercises #1 and use multiplication (instead of repeated addition) to do the examples.

TELLING THE TRUTH ABOUT LONG DIVISION
FACILITY EXERCISES #38

You will be led through some of the long divisions below. A word problem must be made up for each example. Use it to make each step in the long division meaningful. Soon you must do them by yourselves. Check each example. Do not write too large.

(1) $3\overline{)789}$ **Check**	(2) $2\overline{)749}$ **Check**	(3) $78\overline{)420}$ **Check**
(4) $87\overline{)321}$ **Check**	(5) $45\overline{)78}$ **Check**	(6) $37\overline{)9{,}120}$ **Check**

(7) $2\overline{)37}$ Check	(8) $5\overline{)188}$ Check	(9) $24\overline{)14,600}$ Check
(10) $67\overline{)55,917}$ Check	(11) $43\overline{)1,335}$ Check	(12) $54\overline{)4,683}$ Check
(13) $86\overline{)4,683}$ Check	(14) $29\overline{)49}$ Check	(15) $28\overline{)12,231}$ Check

(16) $7\,\overline{)\,56{,}045}$ Check	(17) $368\,\overline{)\,24{,}753}$ Check	(18) $2{,}323\,\overline{)\,9{,}292}$ Check
(19) $8\,\overline{)\,8{,}047}$ Check	(20) $60\,\overline{)\,1{,}823}$ Check	(21) $263\,\overline{)\,987}$ Check
(22) $54\,\overline{)\,20{,}200}$ Check	(23) $4{,}273\,\overline{)\,9{,}867}$ Check	(24) Check

FACILITY EXERCISES #39
Mixed Practice

Write your answers in the spaces provided.

1. Find answers to the examples below without use of fingers.

(a) **17 – 8 + 6 – 7 + 9 – 10 + 5 + 8 – 10 =**________

(b) **5 + 9 + 4 – 8 – 6 + 4 + 7 – 3 + 5 =**________

2. Do the addition and subtraction below. Check the answer to the subtraction.

(a)
$$\begin{array}{r} 7{,}384{,}976 \\ +\ 2{,}615{,}024 \\ \hline \end{array}$$

(b)
$$\begin{array}{r} 1{,}000{,}000 \\ -\quad 590{,}470 \\ \hline \end{array}$$

3. Start at five and count by sixes to sixty-five.

4. Start at four and count by nines to ninety.

5. Start at seventy-six and count backward by sevens to six.

6. Read each numeral below:

(a) **4,001**

(b) **3,000,000,000**

(c) **707,770,077**

7. Name the value of each digit in 270,483,067.

8. Name the value of each place in 270,483,067.

9. The number 700,408,043 is in which

(a) thousands? ____________________

(b) ten-millions? ____________________

(c) hundreds? ____________________

(d) hundred-millions? ____________________

(e) ones? ____________________

(f) ten-thousands? ____________________

(g) millions? ____________________

(h) hundred-thousands? ____________________

(i) tens? ____________________

10. Tell the truth as you do the addition and subtraction example below.

(a)
$$\begin{array}{r} 678,430,825 \\ +\ 625,389,637 \\ \hline \end{array}$$

(b)
$$\begin{array}{r} 540,073,981 \\ -\ 539,175,982 \\ \hline \end{array}$$

11. Find missing numbers.

(a) ________ − 7,648 = 2,753

(b) 671 = 483 + ________

(c) ________ + 697 = 3,001

(d) 67 = 191 − ________

12. Add the following:

$$\begin{array}{r} 673 \\ 47,498 \\ 807 \\ 6,979 \\ 98,568 \\ 746 \\ 79,999 \\ 7,487 \\ 95 \\ 68,960 \\ 9,878 \\ 86,789 \\ 97,597 \\ 54 \\ +\ 678 \\ \hline \end{array}$$

13. Do the following divisions:

a) $4\overline{)27}$ (b) $8\overline{)63}$ (c) $9\overline{)72}$

14. Do the following multiplications:

(a) 74 x 100,000 = ________

(b) 387 x 2,000 = ________

(c) 17 x 10,000 = ________

15. Expand **34 x 526** as a sum of six partial products:

________ + ________ + ________ +

________ + ________ + ________

16. Expand **49 x 83** as a sum of four partial products:

__________ + __________ + __________ + __________

17. Do the following multiplications:

(a) $\begin{array}{r} \mathbf{806} \\ \times\ \mathbf{73} \\ \hline \end{array}$

(b) $\begin{array}{r} \mathbf{5,794} \\ \times\ \mathbf{86} \\ \hline \end{array}$

(c) $\begin{array}{r} \mathbf{7,098} \\ \times\ \mathbf{59} \\ \hline \end{array}$

TELLING THE TRUTH ABOUT LONG DIVISION
FACILITY EXERCISES #40

Do the divisions below. Check each example.

(1) $34\overline{)16,979}$ Check	(2) $499\overline{)16,979}$ Check	(3) $22\overline{)13,058}$ Check
(4) $49\overline{)1,912}$ Check	(5) $493\overline{)4,437}$ Check	(6) $48\overline{)23,700}$ Check

(7)

$46\overline{)364{,}228}$

Check

(8)

$4\overline{)76}$

Check

(9)

$67\overline{)128{,}573}$

Check

(10)

$1{,}919\overline{)128{,}573}$

Check

(11)

$19\overline{)361}$

Check

(12)

$3\overline{)87{,}016}$

Check

(13)

$31 \overline{)901,920}$

Check

(14)

$2,006 \overline{)174,556}$

Check

(15)

$87 \overline{)174,817}$

Check

(16)

$300 \overline{)327,222}$

Check

(17)

$13 \overline{)169}$

Check

(18)

$600 \overline{)32,165}$

Check

(19)

$47 \overline{)140{,}905}$

Check

(20)

$29 \overline{)263{,}755}$

Check

(21)

$36 \overline{)324{,}355}$

Check

(22)

$14 \overline{)5{,}472}$

Check

(23)

$17 \overline{)3{,}396}$

Check

(24)

$19 \overline{)172{,}710}$

Check

(25)

$387 \overline{)742,853}$

Check

(26)

$796 \overline{)556,904}$

Check

(27)

$187 \overline{)16,360}$

Check

(28)

$3,239 \overline{)291,247}$

Check

TELLING THE TRUTH ABOUT LONG DIVISION
FACILITY EXERCISES #41

Do the divisions below without the help of word problems. Check each example.

(1)

$7\overline{)48,003}$

Check

(2)

$49\overline{)2,873}$

Check

(3)

$3\overline{)28,458}$

Check

(4)

$326\overline{)155,433}$

Check

(5)

$8\overline{)4,787}$

Check

(6)

$78\overline{)23,322}$

Check

(7)

$6\overline{)6,059}$

Check

(8)

$24\overline{)10,321}$

Check

(9)

$82\overline{)401,862}$

Check

(10)

$768\overline{)489,489}$

Check

(11)

$9\overline{)72,637}$

Check

(12)

$15\overline{)103,511}$

Check

SOLVING WORD PROBLEMS
FACILITY EXERCISES #42

Do the problems below.

1. Your principal buys 86 workbooks at $7 each and has $4 left. How much money did she start with?

2. If you have $585 and you buy 83 toys at $7 each for your store, how much money would you have left? Could you buy any more toys?

3. If you have $6,438 and you buy 648 toys at $8 each for your store, how much money would you have left? Could you buy any more toys?

4. How many toy cars at $6 each can be bought with $493? How much money is left over?

5. How many tickets for a concert can be bought with $304 if each ticket costs $4? How much money was left?

6. Your father has $270 and buys 9 calculators for his office. How much did he pay for each calculator if they all cost the same amount?

7. If 5 items have been bought from a total of $240, how much was paid for each item if they all cost the same amount?

8. Susan bought 2 handbags for $76. How much did she pay for each if both cost the same amount?

9. Your principal has $25,483. How many workbooks can she buy at $8 each? How much money does she have left?

10. What is the cost of 487 plants at $9 each?

11. How much money would you need to purchase 1,000 calculators at $27 each and 600 chairs at $74 each?

12. If you buy 48 books at $6 each and 54 pens at $3 each, how much money would you spend?

13. If you have $1,500 and you purchase for your store 36 dolls at $5 each, and 96 watches at $9 each, how much money would you have left?

14. Judy has $303. How many puzzles can she buy at $4 each?

15. Henry spends $2,784 to buy 87 model airplanes. If they all cost the same amount of money, how much did each one cost?

16. Mr. Allen bought 9 books for his bookstore. He spent a total of $351. If all the books cost the same amount of money, how much did he pay for each one?

17. You have $200. If you purchase a bike for $87, a pair of skates for $34, a pair of shoes for $29, and a baseball glove for $36, how much money do you have left?

18. Your principal has $986 to spend on items for your school. If she purchases 74 workbooks at $6 each, 68 pens at $2 each, and 82 rulers at $3 each, how much money will she have left? How many boxes of crayons can she now purchase at $3 each?

19. If $981 were spent for the purchase of 9 watches, how much did each watch cost?

20. What is the cost of 600 chairs at $74 each?

21. What is the cost of one thousand calculators at $27 each?

22. Your principal bought 478 notebooks for your school at a cost of $3 each. If he had $1 left over, how much money did he start with?

23. A total of 512 apples have been delivered to a supermarket in 8 boxes. How many apples were there in each box?

24. A total of 2,712 cans of juice have been delivered to a supermarket. If there were 6 cans in each box, how many boxes were there?

25. If you take 849 out of a number 8 times and zero is left, what is that number?

26. If you have $4,353, and you buy as many boxes of candy as you can at $9 each, how much money will you have left?

27. If you take 471 from a number 5 times and there is a remainder of 3, what is that number?

28. Miss Pearson purchases 249 calculators for her store at $38 each. How much money did she spend?

29. If you already have $75 and you sell two radios at $94 each, how much money do you have?

30. If you sell 8 dolls at $34 each and 7 toy cars at $26 each, how much money will you have?

31. If you have $120 and you sell 6 lamps at $47 each and 2 chairs at $24 each, how much money will you have?

32. Mr. Smith bought four cars for his taxi service: the first for $8,000; the second for $9,000; the third for $7,000; the fourth for $12,000. If he had $38,000, how much money does he have left?

33. How many 3's can you take out of 1,976? How much is left over?

34. Janice bought 3 tickets for a concert at $17 each and 5 tickets for a raffle at $8 each. After these tickets were bought, she still had $23 left. How much money did she have at first?

35. How many wheels are there on 236 cars?

36. If you can take a certain number out of 58,482 nine times, what is that number?

37. Bill had $485. He bought 4 shirts at $28 each. With the rest of his money, he bought some pens at $8 each. How many pens did he buy?

38. Miss Jones already has $293. She sells 7 hats at $59 each, 8 wallets at $36 each and 4 radios at $274 each. How much money does Miss Jones have after she made these sales?

39. Miss Pearson purchases 749 calculators for her chain of stores at $38 each and has $29 left over. How much money did she have originally?

40. A furniture store manager has $23,807 with which to purchase sofas at $273 each. How many did she purchase? How much money did she have left? How many pens can she now buy at $2 each?

41. A rent-a-car business purchases 78 cars with a total of $543,504. What is the average cost of each car?

42. Mr. Jones has $2,345 and purchases 69 lamps at $23 each. How much money does he have left over? Did he buy as many lamps as possible? What is the maximum number of lamps he could have bought?

43. Harry Smith bought four different cars for his taxi service: the first for $8,975; the second for $13,897. The third for $17,298; and the fourth for $23,602. If he had $80,000 to spend, how much money was left over?

44. Mrs. Jones bought four of the same type of car at $25,987 each. If she had $120,000 to spend, how much money did she have left?

45. Mr. Cruz bought five different items at a store: the first for $47; the second for $169; the third for $485; the fourth for $236; and the fifth for $97. If he started with $2,000, how much money does he have left?

MULTIPLES
FACILITY EXERCISES #43

List all answers to each example on the line provided. For example:

24 is a multiple of <u>1, 2, 3, 4, 6, 8, 12, 24</u>

(1)

14 is a multiple of______________________________

11 is a multiple of______________________________

6 is a multiple of______________________________

18 is a multiple of______________________________

(2)

34 is a multiple of______________________________

21 is a multiple of______________________________

9 is a multiple of______________________________

36 is a multiple of______________________________

(3)

95 is a multiple of______________________________

25 is a multiple of______________________________

4 is a multiple of______________________________

16 is a multiple of______________________________

(4)

64 is a multiple of______________________________

10 is a multiple of______________________________

81 is a multiple of______________________________

75 is a multiple of______________________________

(5)

54 is a multiple of______________________________

70 is a multiple of______________________________

80 is a multiple of______________________________

72 is a multiple of______________________________

FACTORS
FACILITY EXERCISES #44

Fill in ALL the factors of each number.

	Number	ALL Factors
(1)	20	______
(2)	7	______
(3)	26	______
(4)	31	______
(5)	50	______
(6)	58	______
(7)	66	______
(8)	68	______
(9)	73	______
(10)	76	______
(11)	79	______
(12)	87	______
(13)	88	______
(14)	92	______
(15)	93	______
(16)	98	______
(17)	64	______
(18)	72	______
(19)	96	______
(20)	84	______
(21)	36	______
(22)	120	______
(23)	125	______

FACILITY EXERCISES #45
Mixed Practice

Write your answers in the spaces provided.

1. Find answers to the examples below without use of fingers.

   (a) 8 + 8 + 8 – 6 – 4 – 5 – 3 + 6 + 2 =______

   (b) 7 – 4 + 7 – 3 + 7 – 5 – 2 + 8 – 3 =______

2. Do the addition and subtraction below. Check the answer to the subtraction.

   (a)
   $$\begin{array}{r} 6{,}842{,}937 \\ +\ 6{,}984{,}248 \\ \hline \end{array}$$

   (b)
   $$\begin{array}{r} 69{,}800{,}100 \\ -\ 69{,}429{,}302 \\ \hline \end{array}$$

3. Start at three and count by nines to ninety-three.
4. Start at eight and count forward by tens to one hundred eight.
5. Start at fifty-four and count backward by fives to four.
6. Read each numeral below:

   (a) **513,019**

   (b) **1,000,000,000,000**

7. Name the value of each digit in 111,111,111,111.
8. Name the value of each digit in 111,111,111,111.
9. The number 111,111,111,111 is in which

   (a) ten-billions? ______________________________

   (b) hundred-thousands?______________________________

   (c) millions? ______________________________

   (d) tens? ______________________________

   (e) hundreds? ______________________________

   (f) hundreds millions?______________________________

10. Tell the truth as you do the addition and subtraction examples below.

(a) $\begin{array}{r} 54{,}793{,}628 \\ +\,29{,}154{,}639 \\ \hline \end{array}$

(b) $\begin{array}{r} 54{,}793{,}628 \\ -\,29{,}154{,}639 \\ \hline \end{array}$

11. Find the missing numbers.

(a) **473 = _______ – 945**

(b) **_______ + 40 = 79**

(c) **500 – _______ = 102**

(d) **203 = 73 + _______**

12. Add the following:

$\begin{array}{r} 7{,}438 \\ 796 \\ 584 \\ 9{,}657 \\ 78{,}979 \\ 385 \\ 7{,}867 \\ 794 \\ 678 \\ 948 \\ 85{,}896 \\ 789 \\ 6{,}666 \\ 9{,}577 \\ 58{,}428 \\ 999 \\ +\quad 8{,}865 \\ \hline \end{array}$

13. Do the following divisions:

(a) $3\overline{)\,20}$ (b) $6\overline{)\,54}$ (c) $7\overline{)\,61}$

14. Do the following multiplications:

(a) **57 x 2,000 = _______**

(b) **1,793 x 10,000 = _______**

(c) **9 x 300,000 = _______**

15. Expand **487 x 369** as a sum of nine partial products:

_______ + _______ + _______ +

_______ + _______ + _______ +

_______ + _______ + _______

16. Expand **33 x 333** as a sum of six partial products:

_______ + _______ + _______ + _______ + _______ + _______

17. Do the following multiplications:

(a) $\begin{array}{r} 7{,}090 \\ \times\ 64 \\ \hline \end{array}$

(b) $\begin{array}{r} 7{,}000 \\ \times\ 53 \\ \hline \end{array}$

(c) $\begin{array}{r} 7{,}687 \\ \times\ 36 \\ \hline \end{array}$

18. Do the following divisions:

(a) $57 \overline{)\ 28{,}313}$

(b) $45 \overline{)\ 273{,}193}$

(c) $73 \overline{)\ 65{,}326}$

19. List all numbers of which 80 is a multiple: ______________________

20. Mark has $14,695 and wishes to buy some video games at $38 each. What is the greatest number of games he can buy for his chain of stores?

21. A store owner buys 36 TV sets at $495 each and has $374 left over. How much money did she start with?

22. Can you buy 1,000 cameras at $67 each if you have $105,000?

23. How much does Antonio Gonzalez pay for one lamp if he buys 53 of them for a total of $4,452?

24. George bought 7 shirts at $27 each, 4 trousers at $23 each and 3 pairs of shoes at $35 each. How much money did he spend?

PRIME FACTORIZATION
FACILITY EXERCISES #46

Write the prime factorization of each number in the table below. If the number itself is prime, write "prime number" in the prime factorization column.

	Number	Prime Factorization		Number	Prime Factorization
(1)	20	______	(23)	63	______
(2)	12	______	(24)	65	______
(3)	9	______	(25)	69	______
(4)	81	______	(26)	71	______
(5)	2	______	(27)	57	______
(6)	8	______	(28)	78	______
(7)	18	______	(29)	51	______
(8)	32	______	(30)	85	______
(9)	64	______	(31)	96	______
(10)	25	______	(32)	87	______
(11)	125	______	(33)	88	______
(12)	45	______	(34)	95	______
(13)	42	______	(35)	98	______
(14)	56	______	(36)	100	______
(15)	68	______	(37)	72	______
(16)	37	______	(38)	59	______
(17)	86	______	(39)	120	______
(18)	49	______	(40)	252	______
(19)	51	______	(41)	264	______
(20)	52	______	(42)	245	______
(21)	54	______	(43)	246	______
(22)	60	______	(44)	216	______

FINDING ALL FACTORS OF A NUMBER
FACILITY EXERCISES #47

Fill in the required information for each number in the table below.

	Number	Prime Factorization	ALL Factors
(1)	18		
(2)	28		
(3)	30		
(4)	35		
(5)	36		
(6)	38		
(7)	39		
(8)	40		
(9)	42		
(10)	46		
(11)	47		
(12)	54		
(13)	56		
(14)	60		
(15)	65		
(16)	69		
(17)	70		
(18)	72		
(19)	75		
(20)	80		
(21)	225		
(22)	84		
(23)	216		
(24)	343		
(25)	91		
(26)	308		
(27)	625		

LEAST COMMON MULTIPLE FACILITY EXERCISES #48

In the spaces provided, fill in ten consecutive multiples for each number, six common multiples of each pair and the least common multiple.

Numbers		Consecutive Multiples	Common Multiples	Least Common Multiple
(1)	4			
	6			
(2)	8			
	6			
(3)	5			
	10			
(4)	2			
	5			
(5)	12			
	18			
(6)	20			
	15			
(7)	7			
	21			
(8)	9			
	21			
(9)	4			
	14			

Numbers	Consecutive Multiples	Common Multiples	Least Common Multiple
(10) 30			
6			
(11) 21			
14			
(12) 4			
3			
(13) 24			
8			
(14) 12			
10			
(15) 15			
9			
(16) 6			
9			
(17) 12			
10			
(18) 15			
9			
(19) 8			
14			
(20) 24			
18			

HIGHEST COMMON FACTOR
FACILITY EXERCISES #49

In the spaces provided, fill in all factors for each number, all common factors, and the highest common factor.

Numbers	All Factors	Common Factors	Highest Common Factors
(1) 56			
98			
(2) 96			
40			
(3) 48			
36			
(4) 18			
36			
(5) 90			
42			
(6) 75			
60			
(7) 100			
70			
(8) 54			
45			
(9) 19			
23			
(10) 75			
30			
(11) 14			
28			

Numbers	All Factors	Common Factors	Highest Common Factor
(12) 60			
40			
(13) 7			
21			
(14) 15			
20			
(15) 42			
48			
(16) 84			
105			
(17) 120			
84			
(18) 17			
34			
(19) 31			
47			
(20) 60			
72			

FACILITY EXERCISES #50
Mixed Practice

Write your answers in the spaces provided.

1. Find answers to the examples below without use of fingers.

   (a) **10 + 10 – 8 – 4 + 3 + 7 – 5 – 6 – 7 =_______**

   (b) **7 + 4 – 10 + 9 + 6 – 4 – 2 + 8 – 3 – 1 + 6 =_______**

2. Do the addition and subtraction below. Check the answer to the subtraction.

   (a) $\begin{array}{r} 1,234,567 \\ +\ 9,873,827 \\ \hline \end{array}$

   (b) $\begin{array}{r} 800,010,003 \\ -\ 795,284,372 \\ \hline \end{array}$

3. Start at ninety-three and count backward by tens to three.
4. Start at zero and count by fives to one hundred.
5. Start at five and count by sevens to seventy-five.
6. Read each numeral below:

   (a) **749,413,000,000,000**

   (b) **212,313,414**

7. Name the value of each digit in 483,215,604,019.
8. Name the place value of each digit in 483,215,604,019.
9. The number 87,430 is in which

   (a) ones? ____________________

   (b) hundreds? ____________________

   (c) ten-thousands? ____________________

   (d) thousands? ____________________

   (e) tens? ____________________

10. Tell the truth as you do the addition and subtraction examples below.

   (a) $\begin{array}{r} 4,658,729 \\ +\ 8,594,678 \\ \hline \end{array}$

   (b) $\begin{array}{r} 1,000,000,000 \\ -\qquad 657,047 \\ \hline \end{array}$

11. Find the missing number.

(a) **184 = _______ + 63** (b) **67,498 − _______ = 23,949**

(c) **_______ + 6,784 = 9,231** (d) **954 = _______ − 487**

12. Add the following:

$$\begin{array}{r} 793 \\ 684 \\ 387 \\ 4{,}796 \\ 3{,}847 \\ 87{,}878 \\ 4{,}384 \\ 977 \\ 9{,}486 \\ 95 \\ 6{,}769 \\ 78{,}978 \\ 697 \\ 584 \\ 796 \\ +\ 99{,}999 \\ \hline \end{array}$$

13. Do the following divisions:

a) $8\overline{)\,47}$ (b) $6\overline{)\,48}$ (c) $7\overline{)\,26}$

14. Do the following multiplications:

(a) **71 x 1,000,000 = _______**

(b) **786 x 200 = _______**

(c) **8 x 4,000 = _______**

15. Express **222 x 777** as a sum of nine partial products:

_______ + _______ + _______ +

_______ + _______ + _______ +

_______ + _______ + _______

16. Express **17 x 53** as a sum of four partial products:

__________ + __________ + __________ + __________

17. Do the following multiplications:

(a) $\begin{array}{r} 6{,}700 \\ \times\ 28 \\ \hline \end{array}$ (b) $\begin{array}{r} 8{,}436 \\ \times\ 47 \\ \hline \end{array}$ (c) $\begin{array}{r} 578 \\ \times\ 65 \\ \hline \end{array}$

18. Do the following divisions:

(a) $28\overline{)1{,}751}$ (b) $86\overline{)599{,}493}$ (c) $49\overline{)87{,}857}$

19. List all the numbers of which 112 is a multiple: ____________________

20. List all factors of 100: ____________________

21. Express 240 as a product of prime factors: ____________________

22. Find the least common multiple of 8 and 14.

23. Find the highest common factor of 60 and 48.

24. Miss Simpson has \$5,615 and wishes to buy some tables at \$83 each. What is the largest number of tables she can buy?

25. If Mr. Williams buys 78 radios at \$56 each and has \$43 left over, how much money did he start with?

26. Can the school board buy 10,000 books at \$16 each if they have \$8,500?

27. Mrs. Rivera has \$1,000 and buys 25 dresses (all at the same price) for her daughters. How much did she pay for each one?

28. Olga buys 46 bikes at \$124 each, then 28 pairs of roller skates at \$64 each. If she has \$18 left, how much money did she start with?

USING PRIME FACTORIZATION TO FIND THE L.C.M.
FACILITY EXERCISES #51

Find the L.C.M. for each pair of numbers.

(1) **27 and 45**

(2) **63 and 42**

(3) **50 and 28**

(4) **35 and 49**

(5) **36 and 54**

(6) **48 and 56**

(7) **54 and 48**

(8) **84 and 64**

(9) **15 and 45**

(10) **72 and 84**

(11) **42 and 45**

(12) **27 and 32**

(13) **24 and 36**

(14) **40 and 28**

USING PRIME FACTORIZATION TO FIND THE H.C.F.
FACILITY EXERCISES #52

Learners are to find the H.C.F. for each pair of numbers by means of prime factorization.

(1) **60 and 90**

(2) **120 and 96**

(3) **72 and 96**

(4) **105 and 126**

(5) **116 and 84**

(6) **80 and 100**

(7) **56 and 70**

(8) **78 and 91**

(9) **140 and 84**

(10) **16 and 12**

(11) **48 and 54**

(12) **51 and 85**

(13) **105 and 90**

(14) **120 and 140**

(15) **128 and 96**

(16) **108 and 135**

INTRODUCTION TO FRACTIONS
FACILITY EXERCISES #53

Answer the following questions:

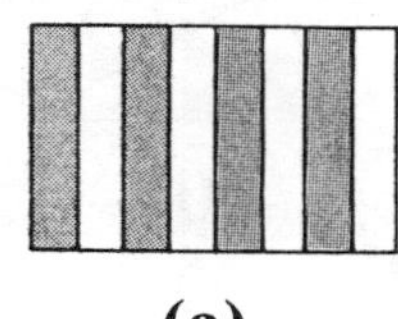
(a)

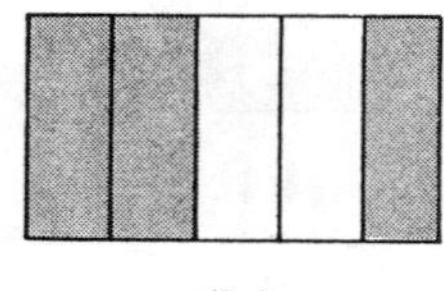
(b)

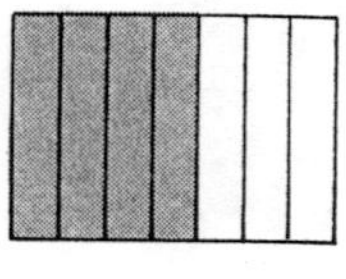
(c)

1. What fraction of rectangle (a) is shaded?
2. What fraction of rectangle (a) is not shaded?
3. What fraction of rectangle (b) is not shaded?
4. What fraction of rectangle (b) is shaded?
5. What fraction of rectangle (c) is not shaded?
6. What fraction of rectangle (c) is shaded?
7. How many eighths are in the whole rectangle (a)?
8. How many fifths are in the whole rectangle (b)?
9. How many sevenths are in the whole rectangle (c)?

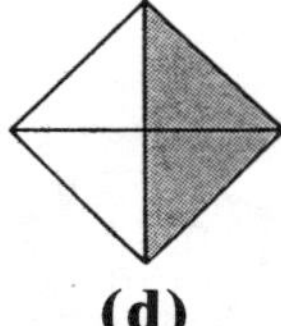
(d)

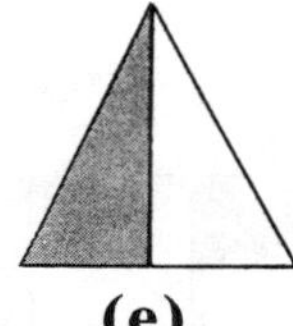
(e)

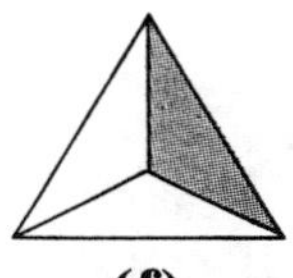
(f)

10. What fraction of figure (d) is shaded?
11. What fraction of figure (d) is not shaded?
12. What fraction of figure (e) is not shaded?
13. What fraction of figure (e) is shaded?
14. What fraction of figure (f) is shaded?
15. What fraction of figure (f) is not shaded?
16. How many fourths are in the whole square (d)?
17. How many halves are in the whole triangle (e)?
18. How many thirds are in the whole triangle (f)?

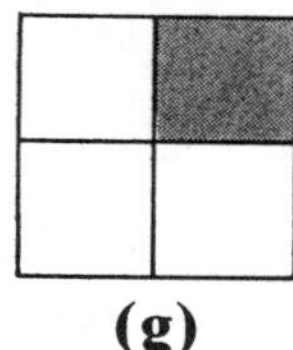
(g)

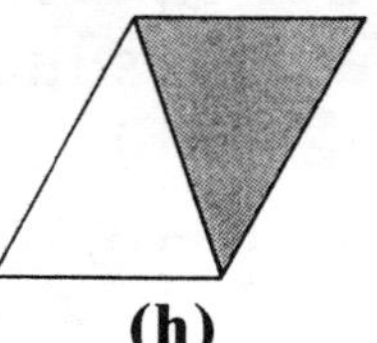
(h)

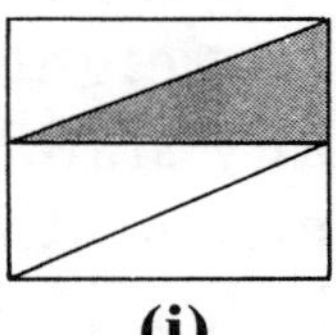
(i)

19. What fraction of figure (g) is not shaded?
20. What fraction of figure (g) is shaded?
21. What fraction of figure (h) is shaded?
22. What fraction of figure (h) is not shaded?
23. What fraction of figure (i) is not shaded?
24. What fraction of figure (i) is shaded?
25. How many fourths are in the whole square (g)?
26. How many halves are in the whole parallelogram (h)?
27. How many fourths are in the whole rectangle (i)?

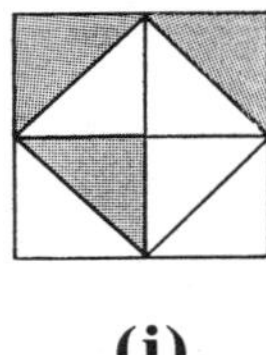
(j)

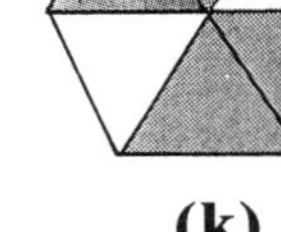
(k)

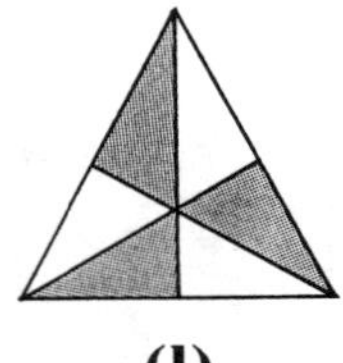
(l)

28. What fraction of figure (j) is not shaded?
29. What fraction of figure (j) is shaded?
30. What fraction of figure (k) is shaded?
31. What fraction of figure (k) is not shaded?
32. What fraction of figure (l) is not shaded?
33. What fraction of figure (l) is shaded?
34. How many eighths are in the whole square (j)?
35. How many sixths are in whole hexagon (k)?
36. How many sixths are in whole triangle (l)?

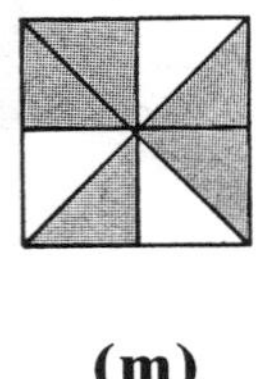
(m)

(n)

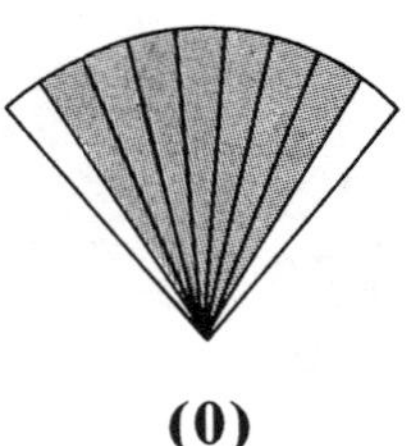
(0)

37. What fraction of figure (m) is shaded?
38. What fraction of figure (m) is not shaded?
39. What fraction of figure (n) is shaded?
40. What fraction of figure (n) is not shaded?
41. What fraction of figure (o) is shaded?
42. What fraction of figure (o) is not shaded?
43. How many eighths are in the whole square (m)?
44. How many sixteenths are in the whole square (n)?
45. How many ninths are in the whole figure (o)?
46. Four wholes, how many thirds?
47. Six wholes, how many fifths?
48. Ten wholes, how many sevenths?
49. Three wholes, how many halves?
50. Eight wholes, how many tenths?

FAMILIES OF EQUIVALENT FRACTIONS
FACILITY EXERCISES #54

Write answers on the lines below the examples.

1. Write the first ten consecutive members of the 3/5 family.

2. Write the first ten consecutive members of the 2/7 family.

3. Write the first ten consecutive members of the 1/8 family.

4. Write the first ten consecutive members of the 1/4 family.

5. Write the first ten consecutive members of the 9/10 family.

6. Write the first ten consecutive members of the 4/5 family.

7. Write the first ten consecutive members of the 3/8 family.

8. Write the first ten consecutive members of the 5/6 family.

9. Write the first ten consecutive members of the 1/3 family.

10. Write the first ten consecutive members of the 8/9 family.

11. Write the first ten consecutive members of the 10/11 family.

12. Write the first ten consecutive members of the 7/12 family.

13. What are the fourths of sixths?

14. Demonstrate that the fourths of sixths are twenty-fourths.

15. What are the halves of sevenths?

16. Demonstrate that the halves of sevenths are fourteenths.

---

17. What are the fifths of thirds?

---

18. Demonstrate that the fifths of thirds are fifteenths.

---

19. Using two rectangles of the same dimentions, show that thirds of fifths are the same size as fifths of thirds.

---

20. Using two rectangles of the same dimensions, show that the fourths of sixths are the same size as sixths of fourths.

---

21. What are the ninths of twenty-thirds?

---

22. What are the sixtieths of forty-sevenths?

---

23. What are the seventy-sixths of fifty-eighths?

---

24. What are the

(a) tenths of tenths?

(b) tenths of hundred-thousandths?

(c) tenths of billionths?

(d) tenths of hundred-millionths?

(e) tenths of hundred-billionths?

(f) tenths of hundredths?

(g) tenths of trillionths?

(h) tenths of ten-thousandths?

(i) tenths of millionths?

(j) tenths of ten-billionths?

(k) tenths of hundred-millionths?

(l) tenths of thousandths?

(m) tenths of hundred-millionths?

---

25. What are the

(a) hundredths of tenths?

(b) thousandths of hundredths?

(c) hundredths of hundredths?

(d) hundredths of thousandths?

(e) thousandths of thousandths?

(f) thousandths of tenths?

FACILITY EXERCISES #55
Mixed Practice

Write your answers in the spaces provided.

1. Find answers to the examples below without use of fingers.

(a) **12 + 4 – 8 – 5 + 3 + 3 – 6 + 7 – 1 =_______**

(b) **5 + 6 + 1 – 7 + 4 + 4 – 9 + 8 + 7 – 10 =_______**

2. Do the addition and subtraction below. Check the answer to the subtraction.

(a)
$$\begin{array}{r} 6{,}954{,}873 \\ +\,3{,}842{,}795 \\ \hline \end{array}$$

(b)
$$\begin{array}{r} 47{,}001{,}001 \\ -\,45{,}842{,}763 \\ \hline \end{array}$$

3. Start at zero and count by elevens to ninety-nine.

4. Start at ninety-one and count backward by nines to one.

5. Start at six and count forward by eights to eighty-six.

6. Read each numeral below:

(a) **21,021,210**

(b) **108,000,015,150,001**

7. Name the value of each digit in 361,413,145,792.

8. Name the place value of each digit in 361,413,145,792.

9. The number 605,065,650 is in which

(a) hundred-thousands?____________________

(b) millions? ____________________

(c) ten-thousands? ____________________

(d) hundreds? ____________________

(e) ten-millions? ____________________

(f) ones? ____________________

(g) thousands? ______

(h) tens? ______

(i) hundred-millions? ______

10. Tell the truth as you do the addition and subtraction examples below.

(a)
```
   7,584,396
+      9,807
```

(b)
```
   1,000,000,000
−         96,438
```

11. Find the missing numbers.

(a) **723 − ______ = 697**

(b) **500 = 101 + ______**

(c) **5 = ______ − 3**

(d) **______ + 59 = 268**

12. Add the following:

```
     738
     495
   8,746
   3,897
  69,879
   4,797
   8,476
  77,999
   9,788
   6,857
  69,469
     878
     465
     793
   4,899
+  7,687
```

13. Do the following divisions:

(a) $4\overline{)31}$ (b) $7\overline{)53}$ (c) $9\overline{)81}$

14. Do the following multiplications:

(a) **1,000 x 10,000 = ______**

(b) **20,000 x 97 = ______**

(c) **40,000 x 196 = ______**

15. Express **439 x 258** as a sum of nine partial products:

______ + ______ + ______ +

______ + ______ + ______ +

______ + ______ + ______

16. Express **63 x 547** as a sum of six partial products:

________ + ________ + ________ + ________ + ________ + ________

17. Do the following multiplications:

(a) $\begin{array}{r} \mathbf{8,070} \\ \times\ \mathbf{38} \\ \hline \end{array}$ (b) $\begin{array}{r} \mathbf{60,000} \\ \times\ \mathbf{84} \\ \hline \end{array}$ (c) $\begin{array}{r} \mathbf{9,876} \\ \times\ \mathbf{67} \\ \hline \end{array}$

18. Do the following divisions:

(a) $\mathbf{453\,\overline{)\,30,526}}$ (b) $\mathbf{97\,\overline{)\,47,807}}$ (c) $\mathbf{492\,\overline{)\,47,807}}$

19. List all numbers of which 90 is a multiple: ______________________

20. List all factors of 128: ______________________

21. Express 225 as a product of prime factors: ______________________

22. Find the least common multiple of 10 and 12.

23. Find the highest common factor of 36 and 90.

24. Use prime factorization to find the least common multiple of 36 and 40.

25. Use prime factorization to find the highest common factor of 84 and 56.

26. How many sevenths are there in 12?

27. Write the first ten consecutive members of the $\frac{4}{9}$ family.

28. Mr. Porter sells 3 used cars at $675 each. With the money he earns from this sale, he buys 6 radios at $36 each, 8 cameras at $42 each and 4 lamps at $54 each. How much money does he have left? With the money left over, how many TV sets can he buy at $167 each?

29. Harry Soto sells his car for $1,350, three sofas at $175 each and five rugs at $188 each. With the money he earns from these sales, how many calculators can he buy for his stores if they cost $48 each? How much money does he have left over?

30. If you have $6,084 and you buy 234 chairs, how much did you pay for each?

31. Can you buy 100 books at $24 each if you have $3,000?

32. Sonia fills 18 boxes with 74 books each and has 20 books left over. How many books did she start with?

FAMILIES OF EQUIVALENT FRACTIONS
FACILITY EXERCISES #56

Fill in the missing space in each row below.

	First Member of Family	Member of Family	Name of this Member
(1)	$\frac{1}{2}$	6th	
(2)	$\frac{5}{9}$	7th	
(3)	$\frac{7}{10}$	4th	
(4)	$\frac{1}{4}$	5th	
(5)	$\frac{1}{2}$		$\frac{9}{18}$
(6)	$\frac{1}{8}$		$\frac{3}{24}$
(7)	$\frac{7}{16}$		$\frac{35}{80}$
(8)		8th	$\frac{40}{64}$
(9)	$\frac{5}{16}$	14th	
(10)		3rd	$\frac{18}{21}$
(11)		10th	$\frac{90}{100}$
(12)		24th	$\frac{24}{48}$
(13)		2nd	$\frac{48}{50}$
(14)	$\frac{7}{8}$		$\frac{84}{96}$
(15)	$\frac{4}{7}$		$\frac{24}{42}$

When the answer to a question below is "yes", state which number of the family is involved.

1. Are there sixteenths in the eighths' family?

2. Are there tenths in the fourths' family?

3. Are there thirtieths in the nineths' family?

4. Are there fortieths in the twentieths' family?

5. Are there seventeenths in the seventeenths' family?

6. Are there fourteenths in the halves' family?

7. Are there thirty-sixths in the fourths' family?

8. Are there twenty-sevenths in the sixths' family?

9. Are there one-hundred-thirty-eighths in the sixths' family?

10. Are there two-hundred-thirty-sixths in the eighths' family?

11. Are there three-hundred-twenty-eighths in the halves' family?

12. Are there eight-hundred-sixteenths in the twenty-fourths' family?

13. Are there hundredths in the tenths' family?

14. Are there millionths in the thousandths' family?

15. Are there ten-thousandths in the hundredths' family?

16. Are there thousandths in the tenths' family?

17. Are there ten-thousandths in the hundredths' family?

18. Are there millionths in the tenths' family?

19. Are there hundred-thousandths in the hundredths' family?

20. Are there millionths in the ten-thousandths' family?

FAMILIES OF EQUIVALENT FRACTIONS
FACILITY EXERCISES #57

Fill in the missing spaces in each row below.

	First Member of Family	Member of Family	Name of this Member
(1)	$\frac{4}{7}$		$\frac{\quad}{35}$
(2)	$\frac{13}{20}$		$\frac{\quad}{180}$
(3)	$\frac{6}{11}$		$\frac{42}{\quad}$
(4)	$\frac{11}{12}$		$\frac{\quad}{108}$
(5)	$\frac{9}{14}$		$\frac{\quad}{70}$
(6)	$\frac{5}{7}$		$\frac{40}{\quad}$
(7)	$\frac{7}{24}$		$\frac{\quad}{72}$
(8)	$\frac{9}{11}$		$\frac{\quad}{11}$
(9)	$\frac{10}{13}$		$\frac{10}{\quad}$
(10)	$\frac{1}{2}$		$\frac{\quad}{92}$
(11)	$\frac{8}{9}$		$\frac{\quad}{72}$
(12)	$\frac{7}{8}$		$\frac{42}{\quad}$
(13)	$\frac{17}{19}$		$\frac{68}{\quad}$
(14)	$\frac{5}{\quad}$		$\frac{15}{42}$
(15)	$\frac{7}{10}$		$\frac{\quad}{1,000}$

	First Member of Family	Member of Family	Name of this Member
(16)	$\frac{93}{100}$		$\frac{\quad}{10{,}000}$
(17)	$\frac{\quad}{10}$		$\frac{9{,}000}{10{,}000}$
(18)	$\frac{\quad}{1{,}000}$		$\frac{48{,}300}{100{,}000}$
(19)	$\frac{37}{100{,}000}$		$\frac{\quad}{1{,}000{,}000}$
(20)	$\frac{3}{100}$		$\frac{\quad}{1{,}000{,}000}$
(21)	$\frac{\quad}{10}$		$\frac{10}{100}$
(22)	$\frac{1}{1{,}000}$		$\frac{\quad}{100{,}000}$
(23)	$\frac{1}{\quad}$		$\frac{1{,}000}{10{,}000}$
(24)	$\frac{17}{100}$		$\frac{17{,}000}{\quad}$
(25)	$\frac{9}{\quad}$		$\frac{900}{1{,}000}$
(26)	$\frac{2{,}943}{10{,}000}$		$\frac{294{,}300}{\quad}$
(27)	$\frac{19}{43}$		$\frac{\quad}{2{,}881}$
(28)	$\frac{71}{231}$		$\frac{17{,}111}{\quad}$

REDUCING FRACTIONS TO LOWEST TERMS
FACILITY EXERCISES #58

Reduce each fraction to lowest terms. Show your work in the space provided.

	Fractions	Show your work
(1)	$\frac{15}{18}$	
(2)	$\frac{16}{24}$	
(3)	$\frac{20}{24}$	
(4)	$\frac{18}{20}$	
(5)	$\frac{12}{18}$	
(6)	$\frac{18}{27}$	
(7)	$\frac{28}{56}$	
(8)	$\frac{28}{42}$	
(9)	$\frac{42}{56}$	
(10)	$\frac{48}{56}$	
(11)	$\frac{42}{48}$	
(12)	$\frac{28}{54}$	
(13)	$\frac{27}{54}$	

REDUCING FRACTIONS TO LOWEST TERMS
FACILITY EXERCISES #59

Reduce to lowest terms by the canceling method.

(1) $\frac{14}{21} =$	(2) $\frac{15}{24} =$	(3) $\frac{40}{50} =$	(4) $\frac{18}{24} =$
(5) $\frac{21}{24} =$	(6) $\frac{16}{48} =$	(7) $\frac{35}{75} =$	(8) $\frac{5}{25} =$
(9) $\frac{5}{10} =$	(10) $\frac{3}{12} =$	(11) $\frac{21}{42} =$	(12) $\frac{9}{54} =$
(13) $\frac{6}{54} =$	(14) $\frac{24}{30} =$	(15) $\frac{18}{54} =$	(16) $\frac{2}{54} =$
(17) $\frac{27}{54} =$	(18) $\frac{8}{56} =$	(19) $\frac{15}{20} =$	(20) $\frac{4}{56} =$
(21) $\frac{14}{56} =$	(22) $\frac{27}{63} =$	(23) $\frac{36}{63} =$	(24) $\frac{16}{64} =$
(25) $\frac{56}{64} =$	(26) $\frac{32}{64} =$	(27) $\frac{64}{72} =$	(28) $\frac{48}{84} =$

(29) $\frac{9}{12} =$ **(30)** $\frac{15}{20} =$ **(31)** $\frac{24}{28} =$ **(32)** $\frac{45}{75} =$

---

(33) $\frac{10}{100} =$ **(34)** $\frac{730}{1{,}000} =$ **(35)** $\frac{300}{10{,}000} =$ **(36)** $\frac{24{,}300}{100{,}000} =$

---

(37) $\frac{100}{10{,}000} =$ **(38)** $\frac{17{,}000}{100{,}000} =$ **(39)** $\frac{90{,}000}{1{,}000{,}000} =$ **(40)** $\frac{5{,}900}{10{,}000} =$

---

(41) $\frac{230}{1{,}000} =$ **(42)** $\frac{1{,}000}{100{,}000} =$ **(43)** $\frac{10}{100{,}000} =$ **(44)** $\frac{748{,}100}{1{,}000{,}000} =$

---

(45) $\frac{100{,}000}{1{,}000{,}000} =$ **(46)** $\frac{70}{100} =$ **(47)** $\frac{6{,}590}{10{,}000} =$ **(48)** $\frac{3{,}000}{100{,}000} =$

REDUCING FRACTIONS TO LOWEST TERMS
FACILITY EXERCISES #60

Reduce to lowest terms by means of prime factorization.

(1) $\frac{56}{64} =$

(2) $\frac{32}{64} =$

(3) $\frac{64}{72} =$

(4) $\frac{48}{84} =$

(5) $\frac{54}{84} =$

(6) $\frac{72}{84} =$

(7) $\frac{72}{96} =$

(8) $\frac{84}{96} =$

(9) $\frac{75}{96} =$

(10) $\frac{54}{75} =$

(11) $\frac{80}{84} =$

(12) $\frac{70}{75} =$

(13) $\frac{288}{432} =$

(14) $\frac{270}{345} =$

(15) $\frac{10}{100} =$

(16) $\frac{100}{1{,}000} =$

(17) $\frac{1{,}000}{10{,}000} =$

(18) $\frac{10{,}000}{100{,}000} =$

(19) $\frac{100{,}000}{1{,}000{,}000} =$

(20) $\frac{100}{10{,}000} =$

(21) $\frac{10}{100{,}000} =$

(22) $\frac{1{,}000}{1{,}000{,}000} =$

(23) $\frac{25}{100} =$

(24) $\frac{75}{100} =$

(25) $\frac{125}{1,000} =$

(26) $\frac{625}{1,000} =$

(27) $\frac{200}{1,000} =$

(28) $\frac{40}{100} =$

(29) $\frac{500}{1,000} =$

(30) $\frac{50}{100} =$

(31) $\frac{8}{10} =$

(32) $\frac{24}{1,000} =$

(33) $\frac{80}{100} =$

(34) $\frac{375}{1,000} =$

(35) $\frac{8}{1,000} =$

(36) $\frac{125}{1,000} =$

(37) $\frac{50}{1,000} =$

(38) $\frac{20}{1,000} =$

(39) $\frac{40}{1,000} =$

(40) $\frac{25}{1,000} =$

(41) $\frac{60}{100} =$

(42) $\frac{75}{1,000} =$

ADDING AND SUBTRACTING WITH FRACTIONS
FACILITY EXERCISES #61

Add or subtract as indicated. Be sure all answers are reduced to lowest terms.

(1) $\frac{5}{8} + \frac{1}{12}$

(2) $\frac{5}{6} - \frac{2}{9}$

(3) $\frac{2}{9} + \frac{2}{3}$

(4) $\frac{7}{10} - \frac{1}{6}$

(5) $\frac{1}{6} + \frac{1}{8}$

(6) $\frac{7}{24} - \frac{1}{8}$

(7) $\frac{7}{24} - \frac{1}{6}$

(8) $\frac{7}{8} + \frac{7}{10}$

(9) $\frac{7}{40} + \frac{7}{10}$

(10) $\frac{7}{8} - \frac{7}{40}$

(11) $\frac{4}{5} - \frac{7}{15}$

(12) $\frac{5}{18} + \frac{1}{6}$

(13) $\frac{3}{4} - \frac{2}{5}$

(14) $\frac{2}{5} + \frac{7}{20}$

(15) $\frac{5}{9} - \frac{2}{9}$

(16) $\frac{2}{9} + \frac{1}{3}$

(17) $\frac{5}{6} - \frac{9}{14}$

(18) $\frac{2}{7} + \frac{1}{2}$

(19) $\frac{11}{14} - \frac{1}{2}$

(20) $\frac{11}{14} - \frac{2}{7}$

(21) $\frac{5}{8} + \frac{1}{8}$

(22) $\frac{3}{4} - \frac{5}{8}$

(23) $\frac{3}{4} - \frac{1}{8}$

(24) $\frac{2}{10} - \frac{2}{15}$

(25) $\frac{1}{3} - \frac{1}{7}$

(26) $\frac{2}{5} + \frac{3}{10}$

(27) $\frac{7}{10} - \frac{2}{5}$

(28) $\frac{7}{10} - \frac{3}{10}$

(29) $\frac{3}{10} + \frac{3}{10}$

(30) $\frac{4}{15} - \frac{1}{5}$

(31) $\frac{1}{6} + \frac{2}{9}$

(32) $\frac{5}{18} - \frac{1}{6}$

(33) $\frac{1}{9} + \frac{1}{6}$

(34) $\frac{2}{7} + \frac{4}{7}$

(35) $\frac{6}{7} - \frac{4}{7}$

(36) $\frac{3}{7} - \frac{1}{21}$

(37) $\frac{5}{6} - \frac{5}{7}$

(38) $\frac{11}{12} - \frac{7}{10}$

(39) $\frac{5}{18} + \frac{7}{18}$

(40) $\frac{1}{8} - \frac{1}{12}$

(41) $\frac{1}{12} + \frac{1}{24}$

(42) $\frac{1}{8} - \frac{1}{24}$

(43) $\frac{2}{9} + \frac{7}{45}$

(44) $\frac{1}{5} + \frac{1}{7}$

(45) $\frac{1}{2} - \frac{3}{7}$

(46) $\frac{1}{14} + \frac{3}{7}$

(47) $\frac{1}{2} - \frac{1}{14}$

(48) $\frac{5}{9} - \frac{3}{8}$

(49) $\frac{5}{7} - \frac{5}{9}$

(50) $\frac{1}{4} + \frac{1}{4}$

(51) $\frac{1}{2} - \frac{1}{4}$

(52) $\frac{5}{12} - \frac{1}{6}$

(53) $\frac{1}{6} + \frac{1}{4}$

(54) $\frac{5}{12} - \frac{1}{4}$

(55) $\frac{2}{15} + \frac{5}{9}$

(56) $\frac{3}{4} - \frac{1}{2}$

(57) $\frac{1}{2} + \frac{1}{4}$

(58) $\frac{3}{4} - \frac{1}{4}$

(59) $\frac{5}{6} - \frac{7}{15}$

(60) $\frac{3}{10} + \frac{7}{15}$

(61) $\frac{3}{8} + \frac{2}{7}$

(62) $\frac{31}{40} - \frac{3}{8}$

(63) $\frac{31}{40} - \frac{2}{5}$

(64) $\frac{11}{28} - \frac{3}{8}$

(65) $\frac{5}{8} - \frac{1}{6}$

(66) $\frac{11}{24} + \frac{1}{6}$

(67) $\frac{5}{8} - \frac{11}{24}$

(68) $\frac{9}{20} + \frac{7}{20}$

(69) $\frac{3}{5} - \frac{9}{20}$

(70) $\frac{3}{20} + \frac{9}{20}$

(71) $\frac{7}{8} - \frac{11}{20}$

(72) $\frac{2}{9} + \frac{5}{12}$

(73) $\frac{13}{36} - \frac{2}{9}$

(74) $\frac{2}{9} + \frac{5}{36}$

(75) $\frac{5}{8} - \frac{3}{10}$

(76) $\frac{3}{10} + \frac{2}{7}$

ADDING AND SUBTRACTING WITH FRACTIONS
FACILITY EXERCISES #62

Do the subtractions below and **check each answer.**

(1) $\frac{9}{14} - \frac{1}{2}$ **Check**

(2) $\frac{7}{8} - \frac{5}{12}$ **Check**

(3) $\frac{5}{8} - \frac{7}{20}$ **Check**

(4) $\frac{13}{15} - \frac{1}{6}$ **Check**

(5) $\frac{9}{13} - \frac{4}{13}$ **Check**

(6) $\frac{11}{14} - \frac{5}{8}$ **Check**

(7) $\frac{5}{12} - \frac{5}{12}$ **Check**

(8) $\frac{17}{36} - \frac{3}{8}$ **Check**

(9) $\frac{5}{9} - \frac{2}{5}$ **Check**

(10) $\frac{29}{30} - \frac{5}{6}$ **Check**

(11) $\frac{39}{41} - \frac{13}{41}$ **Check**

(12) $\frac{3}{8} - \frac{1}{7}$ **Check**

FACILITY EXERCISES #63
Mixed Practice

Write your answers in the spaces provided.

1. Find answers to the examples below without use of fingers.

(a) **18 – 12 + 10 – 13 + 15 – 14 + 11 – 12 + 17 =**_______

(b) **14 – 13 + 15 – 12 + 11 – 14 + 17 – 16 + 18 =**_______

2. Do the addition and subtraction below. Check the answer to the subtraction.

(a)

$$\begin{array}{r} 5{,}498{,}374 \\ +\ 8{,}647{,}253 \\ \hline \end{array}$$

(b)

$$\begin{array}{r} 700{,}003{,}006 \\ -\ 698{,}427{,}507 \\ \hline \end{array}$$

3. Start at zero and count by twelves to one hundred twenty.
4. Start at ninety-eight and count backward by nines to eight.
5. Start at seven and count by eights to eighty-seven.
6. Read each numeral below:

(a) **123,412,341,234**

(b) **123,456,789**

7. Name the value of each digit in 123,412,341,234

8. Name the place vlaue of each digit in 123,412,341,234

9. The number 123,412,341,234 is in which

(a) ten-millions? ____________________

(b) hundreds? ____________________

(c) hundred-thousands? ____________________

(d) billions? ____________________

(e) tens? ____________________

(f) thousands? ____________________

(g) hundred-millions? ____________________

(h) ten-thousands? ____________________

(i) hundred-billions? ____________________

10. Tell the truth as you do the addition and subtraction examples below:

(a)
$$\begin{array}{r} 74{,}985{,}364 \\ +\ 85{,}942{,}697 \\ \hline \end{array}$$

(b)
$$\begin{array}{r} 1{,}000{,}000 \\ -\ \ 87 \\ \hline \end{array}$$

11. Find the missing number.

(a) **888 – _______ = 765**

(b) **69 = 273 – _______**

(c) **743 + _______ = 1,010**

(d) **151 = 34 + _______**

12. Add the following:

$$\begin{array}{r} 6{,}793 \\ 5{,}487 \\ 3{,}845 \\ 7{,}969 \\ 8{,}784 \\ 698 \\ 977 \\ 89{,}475 \\ 4{,}845 \\ 6{,}786 \\ 595 \\ 684 \\ 798 \\ 979 \\ 78{,}867 \\ 7{,}988 \\ 475 \\ +\ \ 568 \\ \hline \end{array}$$

13. Do the following divisions:

(a) $5\overline{)\,49}$ (b) $8\overline{)\,72}$ (c) $6\overline{)\,34}$

14. Do the following multiplications:

(a) **437 x 30,000 = _______**

(b) **85 x 600 = _______**

(c) **7 x 100,000 = _______**

15. Do the following multiplications:

(a)
$$\begin{array}{r} 980 \\ \times\ 48 \\ \hline \end{array}$$

(b)
$$\begin{array}{r} 4{,}008 \\ \times\ 65 \\ \hline \end{array}$$

(c)
$$\begin{array}{r} 798 \\ \times\ 73 \\ \hline \end{array}$$

16. Do the following divisions:

(a) $13\overline{)6{,}443}$ (b) $74\overline{)524{,}808}$ (c) $6{,}072\overline{)261{,}096}$

17. List all numbers of which 140 is a multiple: ______

18. List all factors of 108: ______

19. Express 220 as a product of prime factors: ______

20. Find the least common multiple of 18 and 10. ______

21. Find the highest common factor of 28 and 42. ______

22. Use prime factorization to find the least common multiple of 60 and 48. ______

23. Use prime factorization to find the highest common factor of 120 and 96. ______

24. How many ninths are in 17? ______

25. Write the first ten consecutive members of the $\frac{7}{12}$ family. ______

26. What is the eight member of the $\frac{15}{16}$ family? ______

27. The fraction $\frac{279}{713}$ is what member of the $\frac{9}{23}$ family? ______

28. If $\frac{210}{364}$ is the fourteenth member of a family, what is the first member? ______

29. Reduce $\frac{48}{54}$ to lowest terms. ______

30. Fill in the missing numbers below:

(a) $\frac{17}{32} = \frac{}{256}$ (b) $\frac{6}{} = \frac{90}{105}$ (c) $\frac{7}{18} = \frac{84}{}$

31. Reduce $\frac{105}{150}$ by means of prime factorization. ______________________

32. Subtract the following:

$$\begin{array}{r} \frac{7}{9} \\ -\ \frac{4}{15} \\ \hline \end{array}$$

33. Mr. Rossi has $1,348 and wishes to buy as many books as he can at $39 each. How many did he buy?

34. It takes 86 books to fill one box. How many boxes are need to pack 5,545 books? How many books will be placed in the one unfilled box?

35. Sally Wilson sells 24 paintings at $276 each. She then bought 2 tables at $180 each and 3 sofas at $350 each. With the amount of money left, what is the largest number of radios can she buy at $92 each?

36. How much did you pay for one lamp if 34 of them cost $1,462?

37. Arthur bought 26 plants at $37 each and had $17 left over. How much money did he start with?

37. Erik plans to buy an equal number of bats, balls, mitts and caps which cost $3 each. How many of each can he buy if he uses the amount of money he earns by selling 67 old toys at $2 each at his mother's garage sale?

TRANSFORMING IMPROPER FRACTIONS TO MIXED NUMBERS
FACILITY EXERCISES #64

Transform each improper fraction below to a mixed numeral.

	Improper	Show Your Work In This Column
(1)	$\frac{31}{8}$	
(2)	$\frac{42}{5}$	
(3)	$\frac{17}{6}$	
(4)	$\frac{71}{9}$	
(5)	$\frac{9}{4}$	
(6)	$\frac{43}{8}$	
(7)	$\frac{25}{3}$	
(8)	$\frac{60}{7}$	
(9)	$\frac{97}{10}$	
(10)	$\frac{65}{12}$	
(11)	$\frac{58}{15}$	
(12)	$\frac{61}{23}$	
(13)	$\frac{93}{41}$	
(14)	$\frac{213}{100}$	

TRANSFORMING IMPROPER FRACTIONS TO MIXED NUMBERS
FACILITY EXERCISES #65

Transform the following improper fractions to mixed or whole numbers by means of division.

---

(1) $\frac{83}{10} =$ (2) $\frac{27}{4} =$ (3) $\frac{77}{8} =$ (4) $\frac{59}{13} =$

---

(5) $\frac{74}{21} =$ (6) $\frac{21}{9} =$ (7) $\frac{8}{5} =$ (8) $\frac{42}{7} =$

---

(9) $\frac{97}{43} =$ (10) $\frac{211}{73} =$ (11) $\frac{323}{29} =$ (12) $\frac{77}{3} =$

---

(13) $\frac{25}{18} =$ (14) $\frac{419}{47} =$ (15) $\frac{33}{14} =$ (16) $\frac{100}{81} =$

---

(17) $\frac{99}{98} =$ (18) $\frac{100}{3} =$ (19) $\frac{36}{9} =$ (20) $\frac{43}{14} =$

---

(21) $\frac{57}{19} =$ (22) $\frac{91}{7} =$ (23) $\frac{51}{17} =$ (24) $\frac{73}{7} =$

---

(25) $\frac{41}{2} =$ (26) $\frac{375}{5} =$ (27) $\frac{99}{6} =$ (28) $\frac{847}{300} =$

TRANSFORMING MIXED NUMBERS TO IMPROPER FRACTIONS
FACILITY EXERCISES #66

Transform each mixed numeral to an improper fraction.

Mixed Numeral	Show your work in this column
(1) $4\frac{2}{9}$	
(2) $2\frac{2}{3}$	
(3) $6\frac{1}{4}$	
(4) $1\frac{17}{19}$	
(5) $5\frac{7}{10}$	
(6) $8\frac{7}{13}$	
(7) $6\frac{24}{29}$	
(8) $3\frac{41}{49}$	

TRANSFORMING MIXED NUMBERS TO IMPROPER FRACTIONS
FACILITY EXERCISES #67

Transform each mixed numeral to an improper fraction by means of the short cut.

(1) $2\frac{1}{2} =$ (2) $5\frac{2}{3} =$ (3) $3\frac{4}{5} =$ (4) $8\frac{3}{20} =$

(5) $6\frac{7}{9} =$ (6) $4\frac{1}{4} =$ (7) $13\frac{5}{12} =$ (8) $29\frac{3}{7} =$

(9) $48\frac{5}{8} =$ (10) $16\frac{5}{17} =$ (11) $10\frac{3}{10} =$ (12) $1\frac{3}{5} =$

(13) $7\frac{5}{6} =$ (14) $33\frac{1}{3} =$ (15) $12\frac{4}{7} =$ (16) $4\frac{5}{9} =$

(17) $5\frac{3}{20} =$ (18) $20\frac{3}{4} =$ (19) $1\frac{2}{3} =$ (20) $7\frac{1}{2} =$

(21) $31\frac{1}{8} =$ (22) $18\frac{7}{10} =$ (23) $4\frac{1}{9} =$ (24) $12\frac{7}{8} =$

(25) $45\frac{13}{23} =$ (26) $6\frac{5}{6} =$ (27) $9\frac{1}{9} =$ (28) $25\frac{13}{25} =$

ADDING AND SUBTRACTING WITH MIXED NUMBERS
FACILITY EXERCISES #68

Add or subtract as the sign indicates. Transform all improper fractions to mixed numerals. Be sure all answers are reduced to lowest terms. Check the subtractions.

(1)

$$\begin{array}{r} 6\frac{5}{8} \\ +\ 7\frac{3}{14} \\ \hline \end{array}$$

(2) **Check**

$$\begin{array}{r} 7\frac{5}{6} \\ -\ 2\frac{3}{4} \\ \hline \end{array}$$

(3) **Check**

$$\begin{array}{r} 13\frac{8}{15} \\ -\ 5\frac{2}{9} \\ \hline \end{array}$$

(4)

$$\begin{array}{r} 23\frac{5}{8} \\ +\ 9\frac{11}{20} \\ \hline \end{array}$$

(5)

$$\begin{array}{r} 2\frac{3}{7} \\ +\ 2\frac{3}{7} \\ \hline \end{array}$$

(6) **Check**

$$\begin{array}{r} 4\frac{6}{7} \\ -\ 2\frac{3}{7} \\ \hline \end{array}$$

(7)

$$\begin{array}{r} 8\frac{1}{3} \\ +\ 8\frac{1}{2} \\ \hline \end{array}$$

(8)

$$\begin{array}{r} 6\frac{1}{6} \\ +\ 7\frac{2}{9} \\ \hline \end{array}$$

(9) **Check**

$$\begin{array}{r} 13\frac{7}{18} \\ -\ 6\frac{1}{6} \\ \hline \end{array}$$

(10) **Check**

$$\begin{array}{r} 13\frac{7}{18} \\ -\ 7\frac{2}{9} \\ \hline \end{array}$$

(11)

$$\begin{array}{r} 8\frac{3}{10} \\ +\ 7\frac{2}{15} \\ \hline \end{array}$$

(12) **Check**

$$\begin{array}{r} 15\frac{13}{30} \\ -\ 7\frac{2}{15} \\ \hline \end{array}$$

(13) Check

$$15\frac{13}{30} - 8\frac{3}{10}$$

(14) Check

$$16\frac{7}{12} - 5\frac{2}{9}$$

(15) Check

$$1\frac{3}{4} - 1\frac{9}{10}$$

(16) Check

$$9\frac{7}{12} - \frac{3}{10}$$

(17)

$$35\frac{3}{8} + 29\frac{5}{24}$$

(18) Check

$$64\frac{7}{12} - 29\frac{5}{24}$$

(19)

$$8\frac{5}{17} + 2\frac{7}{17}$$

(20)

$$23\frac{3}{14} + 5\frac{3}{4}$$

(21) Check

$$28\frac{27}{28} - 23\frac{3}{14}$$

(22) Check

$$28\frac{27}{28} - 5\frac{3}{4}$$

(23) Check

$$8\frac{9}{10} - 8\frac{5}{6}$$

(24)

$$9\frac{13}{15} + 9\frac{3}{5}$$

(25) Check

$$5\frac{3}{4} - 2\frac{1}{2}$$

(26)

$$15\frac{1}{6} + 2\frac{7}{20}$$

(27) Check

$$19\frac{17}{18} - 7\frac{3}{4}$$

(28)

$$\begin{array}{r} 1\frac{1}{2} \\ +\ 1\frac{1}{2} \\ \hline \end{array}$$

(29)

$$\begin{array}{r} 9\frac{3}{5} \\ -\ 2\frac{1}{3} \\ \hline \end{array}$$

Check

(30)

$$\begin{array}{r} \frac{5}{6} \\ +\ 30\frac{7}{10} \\ \hline \end{array}$$

(31)

$$\begin{array}{r} 5\frac{1}{2} \\ +\ 5\frac{1}{7} \\ \hline \end{array}$$

(32)

$$\begin{array}{r} 10\frac{9}{14} \\ -\ 5\frac{1}{7} \\ \hline \end{array}$$

Check

(33)

$$\begin{array}{r} 3\frac{13}{15} \\ +\ 3\frac{7}{10} \\ \hline \end{array}$$

(34)

$$\begin{array}{r} 6\frac{4}{9} \\ +\ 6\frac{4}{9} \\ \hline \end{array}$$

(35)

$$\begin{array}{r} 12\frac{5}{14} \\ -\ 6\frac{1}{6} \\ \hline \end{array}$$

Check

(36)

$$\begin{array}{r} 7\frac{2}{3} \\ +\ 2\frac{1}{3} \\ \hline \end{array}$$

(37)

$$\begin{array}{r} 1\frac{3}{4} \\ +\ \frac{1}{4} \\ \hline \end{array}$$

(38)

$$\begin{array}{r} 8\frac{2}{3} \\ +\ 5\frac{3}{4} \\ \hline \end{array}$$

(39)

$$\begin{array}{r} 2\frac{1}{9} \\ +\ 1\frac{1}{8} \\ \hline \end{array}$$

(40)

$$\begin{array}{r} \frac{5}{7} \\ -\ \frac{4}{9} \\ \hline \end{array}$$

Check

(41)

$$\begin{array}{r} \frac{1}{7} \\ +\ \frac{1}{56} \\ \hline \end{array}$$

(42)

$$\begin{array}{r} \frac{37}{461} \\ +\ \frac{159}{461} \\ \hline \end{array}$$

TRANSFORMING MIXED NUMBERS
FACILITY EXERCISES #69

Fill in the missing numerators and denominators. Explain your answers.

(1) $6\frac{7}{8} = 5\frac{}{}$ —

(2) $7\frac{4}{7} = 6$ —

(3) $1\frac{7}{10} =$ —

(4) $4\frac{3}{8} = 3$ —

(5) 5 — $= 4\frac{11}{8}$

(6) $2\frac{7}{16} = 1$ —

(7) 8 — $= 7\frac{147}{100}$

(8) $15\frac{5}{12} = 14$ —

(9) 3 — $= 2\frac{121}{84}$

(10) $9\frac{1}{2} = 8$ —

(11) 13 — $= 12\frac{33}{32}$

(12) $19\frac{3}{4} = 18$ —

(13) 5 — $= 4\frac{9}{7}$

(14) $1\frac{1}{2} =$ —

(15) 10 — $= 9\frac{13}{8}$

(16) $2\frac{153}{286} = 1$ —

(17) 13 — $= 12\frac{109}{96}$

(18) $17\frac{9}{17} = 16$ —

(19) 5 — $= 4\frac{67}{36}$

(20) $7\frac{171}{488} = 6$ —

(21) $8\frac{29}{64} = 7$ —

"EXCHANGE" IN SUBTRACTION WITH MIXED NUMBERS
FACILITY EXERCISES #70

Do the subtractions below. Be sure all answers are reduced to lowest terms. Check all subtractions.

(1) **Check**

$$\begin{array}{r} 7\frac{2}{9} \\ -\ 2\frac{5}{6} \\ \hline \end{array}$$

(2) **Check**

$$\begin{array}{r} 5\frac{3}{4} \\ -\ 1\frac{5}{6} \\ \hline \end{array}$$

(3) **Check**

$$\begin{array}{r} 23\frac{7}{10} \\ -\ 7\frac{3}{8} \\ \hline \end{array}$$

(4) **Check**

$$\begin{array}{r} 5\frac{2}{19} \\ -\ 4\frac{10}{19} \\ \hline \end{array}$$

(5) **Check**

$$\begin{array}{r} 13\frac{5}{24} \\ -\ 6\frac{7}{12} \\ \hline \end{array}$$

(6) **Check**

$$\begin{array}{r} 25\frac{1}{8} \\ -\ 7\frac{1}{4} \\ \hline \end{array}$$

(7) **Check**

$$\begin{array}{r} 1\frac{1}{27} \\ -\ \frac{5}{9} \\ \hline \end{array}$$

(8) **Check**

$$\begin{array}{r} 18\frac{3}{4} \\ -\ 7\frac{11}{14} \\ \hline \end{array}$$

(9) **Check**

$$\begin{array}{r} 9\frac{1}{4} \\ -\ 2\frac{1}{2} \\ \hline \end{array}$$

(10) **Check**

$$\begin{array}{r} 9\frac{1}{3} \\ -\ 2\frac{3}{5} \\ \hline \end{array}$$

(11) **Check**

$$\begin{array}{r} 15\frac{1}{6} \\ -\ 2\frac{7}{20} \\ \hline \end{array}$$

(12) **Check**

$$\begin{array}{r} 6\frac{9}{40} \\ -\ 3\frac{4}{5} \\ \hline \end{array}$$

ADDING AND SUBTRACTING WITH FRACTIONS AND MIXED NUMBERS
FACILITY EXERCISES #71

Add or subtract as indicated. Space is provided below each problem for finding the L.C.D. by means of prime factorization (where necessary). Transform all improper fractions to mixed numerals and, if possible, reduce the answer to lowest terms.

(1) $\frac{7}{24} + \frac{5}{56}$

(2) $\frac{3}{50} + \frac{11}{15}$

(3) $\frac{19}{36} - \frac{7}{45}$ **Check**

(4) $\frac{39}{40} - \frac{49}{60}$ **Check**

(5) $\frac{31}{54} + \frac{43}{60}$

(6) $\frac{29}{60} - \frac{3}{56}$ **Check**

(7) $\frac{7}{24} + \frac{23}{54}$

(8) $\frac{41}{45} + 2\frac{33}{50}$

(9) $4\frac{7}{20} - 3\frac{5}{12}$ **Check**

(10) $7\frac{19}{24} - \frac{7}{18}$ **Check**

(11) $4\frac{17}{24} + 5\frac{9}{16}$

(12) $6\frac{13}{20} + \frac{21}{25}$

(13) $6\frac{5}{27} - 1\frac{11}{18}$ **Check**

(14) $13\frac{7}{24} - 8\frac{23}{20}$ **Check**

(15) $6\frac{7}{24} - \frac{3}{5}$ **Check**

(16)

$$\begin{array}{r} 6 \\ +\ \frac{3}{5} \\ \hline \end{array}$$

(17) **Check**

$$\begin{array}{r} 1 \\ -\ \frac{2}{15} \\ \hline \end{array}$$

(18) **Check**

$$\begin{array}{r} 1\frac{1}{2} \\ -\ \frac{3}{4} \\ \hline \end{array}$$

(19)

$$\begin{array}{r} 8\frac{2}{5} \\ +\ 8\frac{3}{5} \\ \hline \end{array}$$

(20)

$$\begin{array}{r} \frac{3}{8} \\ +\ 6\frac{2}{9} \\ \hline \end{array}$$

(21) **Check**

$$\begin{array}{r} 7\frac{9}{38} \\ -\ 7 \\ \hline \end{array}$$

(22) **Check**

$$\begin{array}{r} 73\frac{25}{48} \\ -\ \frac{25}{48} \\ \hline \end{array}$$

(23)

$$\begin{array}{r} 10\frac{19}{24} \\ +\ 7\frac{20}{27} \\ \hline \end{array}$$

(24)

$$\begin{array}{r} 2\frac{5}{28} \\ +\ 3\frac{3}{20} \\ \hline \end{array}$$

(25) **Check**

$$\begin{array}{r} 8\frac{1}{4} \\ -\ \frac{1}{2} \\ \hline \end{array}$$

(26) **Check**

$$\begin{array}{r} \frac{6}{7} \\ -\ \frac{3}{4} \\ \hline \end{array}$$

(27)

$$\begin{array}{r} \frac{1}{2} \\ +\ \frac{1}{5} \\ \hline \end{array}$$

(28)

$$\begin{array}{r} \frac{1}{3} \\ +\ \frac{1}{6} \\ \hline \end{array}$$

(29) **Check**

$$\begin{array}{r} 1\frac{1}{7} \\ -\ \frac{1}{2} \\ \hline \end{array}$$

(30) **Check**

$$\begin{array}{r} \frac{1}{2} \\ -\ \frac{1}{3} \\ \hline \end{array}$$

(31) **Check**

$$\begin{array}{r} 18\frac{7}{19} \\ -\ 17\frac{10}{19} \\ \hline \end{array}$$

(32) $26\frac{7}{30} - 8\frac{7}{15}$

Check

(33) $\frac{3}{8} + \frac{5}{8}$

(34) $\frac{3}{11} + \frac{5}{11}$

(35) $3\frac{7}{16} + 2\frac{11}{12}$

(36) $3\frac{7}{16} - 2\frac{11}{12}$

Check

(37) $6\frac{8}{9} - 2$

Check

(38) $1 - \frac{2}{5}$

Check

(39) $85 - 3\frac{15}{16}$

Check

(40) $21\frac{9}{24} - \frac{9}{14}$

Check

(41) $\frac{1}{2} + \frac{1}{2}$

(42) $15 - \frac{1}{9}$

Check

(43) $73\frac{19}{52} - 73$

Check

(44) $7\frac{1}{45} + 8\frac{1}{60}$

(45) $26\frac{7}{36} - 5\frac{25}{42}$

Check

(46) $\frac{5}{72} + \frac{7}{90}$

(47) $8\frac{17}{144} + 2\frac{57}{120}$

FACILITY EXERCISES #72
Mixed Practice

Write your answers in the spaces provided.

1. Find the answers to the examples below without use of fingers.

(a) **19 – 15 + 13 – 10 + 12 – 15 + 12 – 13 + 14 – 12 =** ________

(b) **17 – 14 + 12 – 11 + 13 – 15 + 17 – 16 + 15 – 10 + 8 =** ________

2. Do the addition and subtraction below. Check the answer to the subtraction.

(a)
$$\begin{array}{r} 10{,}010{,}001 \\ -\ \ 8{,}513{,}062 \\ \hline \end{array}$$

(b)
$$\begin{array}{r} 5{,}493{,}786 \\ -\ 5{,}947{,}272 \\ \hline \end{array}$$

3. Start at zero and count by thirteens to one hundred thirty.

4. Start at seven and count by eights to eighty-seven.

5. Start at sixty-one and count backward by fours to one.

6. Read each numeral below:

(a) **1,235,512,345**

(b) **5,000,000,050**

7. Name and write the value of each digit in 1,234,512,345.

8. Name and write the place value of each digit in 1,234,512,345.

9. The number 1,234,512,345 is in which

(a) ten-millions? ________________

(b) hundreds? ________________

(c) hundred-thousands? ________________

(d) billions? ________________

(e) tens? ________________

(f) thousands? ________________

(g) hundred-millions? ________________

(h) ten-thousands? ________________

10. Tell the truth as you do the addition and subtraction examples below:

(a)
$$\begin{array}{r} 65{,}728{,}493 \\ +\ 75{,}801{,}674 \\ \hline \end{array}$$

(b)
$$\begin{array}{r} 1{,}000{,}000{,}000 \\ -\ \quad 69{,}506 \\ \hline \end{array}$$

11. Find the missing number:

(a) 5,487 – _______ = 1,989

(b) _______ + 987 = 3,051

(c) 28,471 = _______ – 7,979

(d) 31 = 19 + _______

12. Add the following:

$$\begin{array}{r} 649 \\ 5{,}984 \\ 7{,}878 \\ 9{,}797 \\ 86{,}475 \\ 3{,}234 \\ 7{,}658 \\ 4{,}936 \\ 875 \\ 9{,}768 \\ 46{,}999 \\ 94{,}853 \\ 7{,}678 \\ 8{,}586 \\ 76{,}969 \\ 743 \\ 876 \\ +\ \quad 945 \\ \hline \end{array}$$

13. Do the following divisions:

(a) $3\overline{)17}$ (b) $8\overline{)71}$ (c) $7\overline{)56}$

14. Do the following multiplications:

(a) 68 x 50 = _______

(b) 864 x 100,000 = _______

(c) 6 x 70,000 = _______

15. Do the following multiplications:

(a)
$$\begin{array}{r} 47{,}600 \\ \times\ 470 \\ \hline \end{array}$$

(b)
$$\begin{array}{r} 23{,}000 \\ \times\ 690 \\ \hline \end{array}$$

(c)
$$\begin{array}{r} 798{,}000 \\ \times\ 6{,}700 \\ \hline \end{array}$$

16. Do the division examples below:

(a) $4{,}352\,\overline{)\,281{,}291}$

(b) $576\,\overline{)\,10{,}113}$

(c) $300\,\overline{)\,20{,}697}$

17. List all numbers of which 324 is a multiple: ____________________

18. List all factors of 150: ____________________

19. Express 104 as a product of primes: ____________________

20. Find the least common multiple of 16 and 24. ____________________

21. Find the highest common factor of 32 and 48. ____________________

22. Use prime factorization to find the least common multiple of 75 and 90. ________

23. Use prime factorization to find the highest common factor of 378 and 180. ________

24. How many fifths are there in 16? ____________

25. Write the first ten consecutive numbers of the $\frac{11}{14}$ family. ____________________

26. What is the sixth member of the $\frac{14}{15}$ family? ____________________

27. The fraction $\frac{63}{117}$ is which member of the $\frac{7}{13}$ family? ____________________

28. If $\frac{90}{105}$ is the fifteenth member of a family, what is the first member? ________

29. Reduce $\frac{24}{36}$ to lowest tems. ______________

30. Fill in the missing numbers below:

(a) $\frac{3}{8} = \frac{\quad}{32}$ (b) $\frac{6}{7} = \frac{36}{\quad}$ (c) $\frac{\quad}{4} = \frac{21}{28}$

31. Reduce $\frac{180}{324}$ by means of prime factorization. ______________________________

32. Add the following:

$$\begin{array}{r} \frac{3}{14} \\ + \ \frac{5}{8} \\ \hline \end{array}$$

33. Transform $\frac{53}{8}$ to a mixed number. ______________________________

34. Transform $7\frac{5}{9}$ to an improper fraction. ______________________________

35. Add:

$$\begin{array}{r} 8\frac{11}{12} \\ + \ 5\frac{7}{9} \\ \hline \end{array}$$

36. Subtract:

Check

$$\begin{array}{r} 7\frac{2}{15} \\ - \ 5\frac{7}{10} \\ \hline \end{array}$$

37. Add:

$$\begin{array}{r} 14\frac{51}{72} \\ + \ 9\frac{31}{54} \\ \hline \end{array}$$

38. Subtract:

Check

$$\begin{array}{r} 23\frac{17}{40} \\ - 16\frac{73}{90} \\ \hline \end{array}$$

39. One crate holds 42 oranges. How many crates are needed for 2,814 oranges?

40. Edward bought 7 tickets for a baseball game at $57 each and 14 tickets for a raffle at $24 each. After these tickets were bought, he still had $16 left. How much money did he have at first?

41. James Allen sells 94 watches at $136 each. With the money earned, he bought 3 TV sets at $345 each and decided to buy as many calculators as he could at $35 each. How many calculators did he buy?

42. How much money did you start with if you bought 18 toys at $28 each and had $3 left?

43. Veda wishes to buy an equal number of blue and white shirts. If both shirts cost $18 each, how many can she buy if she has $1,437?